MANHATTAN STYLE

MANHATTAN STYLE

BY
JOHN ESTEN
WITH
ROSE BENNETT GILBERT

PHOTOGRAPHS
BY
GEORGE CHINSEE

LITTLE, BROWN AND COMPANY

BOSTON · TORONTO · LONDON

TO
STANLEY BARROWS
FOR
HIS KNOWLEDGE, INSPIRATION,
AND INFLUENCE
ON
MANHATTAN STYLE

Endpapers:
A parchment-covered Parsons table
by Jean-Michel Frank,
from the collection of Gary Hager.
Dimensions: height, 16"; width, 31"; depth, 15½"

Frontispiece:
Reflecting on the past, designer Gary Hager of Parish-Hadley Associates recreates the "luxury of simplicity" that characterized the work of Jean-Michel Frank. The carved and gilt wooden mirror is after a Frank original; the head on the limestone chimneypiece was carved in the 1920s by the Russian artist Sonia Brown.

Page viii:
A keen sense of the past lends presence to a contemporary penthouse designed by John Saladino. A painter and architect as well as a designer, Saladino orchestrates a cool blend of iridescent colors, furniture of his own design, and art. The sculpture at left is *Untitled Small Stack* by Donald Judd.

FIRST EDITION

Library of Congress Cataloging-in-Publication Data

Esten, John.
    Manhattan style/by John Esten with Rose Gilbert;
photographs by George Chinsee.
    p. cm.
    1. Interior decoration — New York (N.Y.) — History — 20th
century. 2. Apartments — New York (N.Y.) I. Gilbert, Rose
Bennett. II. Title.
NK2004.E86 1990
747'.88314'097471 — dc20   90-6024

10 9 8 7 6 5 4 3 2 1

Published simultaneously in Canada
by Little, Brown & Company (Canada) Limited

PRINTED IN JAPAN

CONTENTS

ACKNOWLEDGMENTS

The preparation of this book has been a real group effort in every respect. From concept to completion, many people have helped in many ways — some with scholarship, some with personal experiences or memories, and others with kindness, patience, and their valuable time.

One of the more pleasant aspects of this "effort" was working with George Chinsee, whose eye and taste have resulted in these superb photographs, made in some cases under unusual conditions. We could write another book relating some of our experiences. There was, for instance, the morning at Mrs. Parish's apartment when the burglar alarm suddenly went off for no apparent reason, and Mrs. Parish's French housekeeper, who doesn't speak English, and I, who in the best of circumstances can't *parler* very well, tried to find it and turn it off before the police arrived. We did, they didn't, and George got the picture. The photographs look *very* serene, too. Giovanni de Moura, George's assistant, was with us every day, all the way.

Rose Gilbert's part in this work has always seemed to be effortless; the research we did together, along with interviews of the people included in the book, always sparkled with her enthusiasm, and the result is this spirited text. (Rose, *I* know it wasn't effortless!)

Stanley Barrows's knowledge, inspiration, and influence on generations of students at the Parsons School and the Fashion Institute of Technology are not only an integral part of the design movement that this book encompasses but have contributed greatly to this work.

Our hats are off to Pauline Metcalf, upon whose research and scholarship on Ogden Codman, Jr., we have drawn generously. It was her insight that first redefined Codman from a footnote to a major innovator of American design in this century.

A great portion of this book consists of work by designers who are productive today. Along with their choices of those examples of their oeuvre which they wanted to include in the book, I have always opted to photograph their personal environments. A designer's own home, I feel, best expresses his or her individuality without the constraint of pleasing the client — however necessary that fact of life might be!

I am indeed grateful to the designers and their clients, along with other trendsetters who allowed us to photograph their homes or apartments and who graciously endured the disruption that always entails. I would like to thank not only the designers but some of the members of their design teams who assisted us: *Thomas Britt, Incorporated:* Peter Napolitano and Malcolm McKinstrie; *Dorothy Draper, Incorporated:* Nellie Xinos; *Melvin Dwork, Incorporated:* Dana Nicholson; *David Anthony Easton, Incorporated:* Katie True and John Christenson; *André Emmerich Gallery, Incorporated:* Dorsey Waxter; *Mark Hampton, Incorporated:* Louise Cursio; *McMillen, Incorporated:* Betty Sherrill, Brooks Anderson, John Drews, and Luis Rey; *Kevin McNamara, Incorporated:* Thomas Jayne; *Parish-Hadley Associates:* Diane Miller; *Renny:* Pat McCoy; *John F. Saladino, Incorporated:* Jane Seaman; *Garrick C. Stephenson, Incorporated:* Eduardo Hernandez.

In addition, Pat Coman of the Thomas J. Watson Library; Andrea Bayer of the Photography and Print Department and Mary Dougherty of the Photograph and Slide Library at the Metropolitan Museum of Art; Dale Neighbors of the New York Historical Society; Tony Wren of the National Institute of Architects; Sharon Chickanzeff and Howard Wood of the Parsons Library; Robert H. Montgomery, Jr., and Florence Leeds of the Cole Porter Trust; Ronald Grimaldi of Rose Cumming, Incorporated; Carleton Varney of Dorothy Draper, Incorporated; Cynthia Cathcart, Margaret Morse, Annette Ohnikian, and especially Diana Edkins of Condé Nast Publications; Thomas Beaton, Miki Denhof, Rose Gottschalk, Eve Gromek, Lizzie Himmel, Brian Johnson, Ruth Mueller, Edgar Munhall, Frank Randolph, Mrs. Nelson Rockefeller, and Ann Sonet have greatly contributed to this book in a variety of ways.

In other very special ways, our editors, experts, and friends at Little, Brown and Company have helped make this work a reality: James Collins, Dana Groseclose, Christina Eckerson, Dorothy Straight, and, in particular, Ray Roberts.

After all, this "effort" brings to mind Montaigne, who once wrote, "The journey, not the arrival, matters."

John Esten

PREFACE

Energy, variety, and constant change exemplify life in Manhattan. Juxtaposed between two rivers, in an amazing conglomeration of architecture, live not only native New Yorkers but also the creative and the talented who have emigrated from other parts of America and diverse areas of the globe.

This mix of the native and the transplanted triggers a continual flow of new ideas, inspiring an eclectic decorative style that has become indigenous to New York and is recognized far beyond the city's sky-scraping apartments, vintage town houses, and lofts. Whether it turns up in a forty-five-story-high penthouse along the East River or in a Greenwich Village studio, the look is easy to recognize. Let's call it Manhattan Style.

Manhattan Style is not about period rooms filled with traditional furniture and antiques. Rather, it is a combination of many periods, often including the very new, sometimes assembled in hard-edged, contemporary, boxlike spaces. What it *is* about, without question, is antiques and art, both the old masters and the new young Turks of the avant garde. However, there are other, more individual aspects to the look, as well. Manhattan Style is also history. To trace its evolution is to document the development of interior design as we know it today. The very idea was born here, in the providential literary collaboration of a young Boston architect, Ogden Codman, Jr., and an uncommitted writer who would go on to become a major American literary figure, Edith Wharton. The book they wrote together, *The Decoration of Houses*, encouraged Americans to rethink the dark, overstuffed rooms in which they were then living. The year was 1897; Victorian taste was still very much in evidence, with its upright horsehair upholstery, its multilayered Turkish carpets, and its predictable potted palms.

What Codman and Mrs. Wharton urged — a return to clean, classic lines and simplified living spaces — New York–born Elsie de Wolfe soon put into practice. An erstwhile actress whose personal style, if not her dramatic talents, put her on top, de Wolfe had the savvy to engage Ogden Codman to help her redecorate her houses. Ultimately this influenced her decision to retire from acting and establish herself as the first professional decorator anywhere.

Others came quick and thick on her heels, names that make up the history of interior design. Among them was Ruby Ross Wood, who ghostwrote Elsie de Wolfe's *The House in Good Taste* and went on to practice those ideas herself. One of the many she influenced was a young Baltimore-born designer named Billy Baldwin, still celebrated for his love of the simple and the sensible. Looking back on his career in design, Billy once wrote, "I am nearly as old as American decorating itself — this makes me one of the few decorators alive who has seen the germination, cultivation, weeding, and flowering of decorating in this country."

The list goes on, recalling the talents who flourished in New York and who are still influencing designers two generations later: Rose Cumming, known for her eccentric taste and vibrant use of color; Syrie Maugham, who from her Fifty-seventh Street shop painted the town white; Frank Alvah Parsons, president of Parsons, the first school to teach interior design as a profession; William Odom, who never decorated professionally (he could not tolerate working with clients) but who eventually became president of the Parsons School; Van Day Truex, the next president of Parsons (later the design director of Tiffany & Company), who taught hundreds of young designers to understand classic architecture and design. Truex was also the conduit through which America met the colossal French talent Jean-Michel Frank, the man who fashioned himself an "interior eliminator."

Then there were Dorothy Draper, who brought comfort to America's hotels and comforting words to America's homemakers through her magazine and newspaper columns; Mrs. Archibald Brown, the founder of McMillen, Inc., a pioneer and design counsel to generations of American gentry; Mrs. Henry Parish II — Sister Parish — of Parish-Hadley, still setting trends after a half century in business.

This magical mixture of tastemakers and their modern-day heirs — artists, designers, and art and antique dealers as well as fabric, furniture, and flower designers (who, as Syrie Maugham often said, add the icing to a room) — is what we have culled from the crazy paradise of architecture, interiors, and life-styles assembled in a big city on a small island like no other: Manhattan.

John Esten

MANHATTAN STYLE

They moved in the same rarefied circles of society, saw — and disdained — the same overwrought ornamentation in the rooms through which they passed. So it was that nearly a century ago, two people of like mind sat down together to collaborate on an unlikely project.

He was the quintessential Boston Brahmin: haughty, obsessed with genealogy, he had lived and studied in Europe, was already winning acclaim for his architectural work, and had shrewdly spread his practice to New York, where there were more clients who could — and would — pay for his services. She was the crème of New York society, locked in an unhappy marriage, recovering from a nervous collapse, a dilettante who was just developing an appreciation for classical architecture and the decorative arts, yet to realize her future as a great writer.

The book they wrote together, *The Decoration of Houses,* was Edith Wharton's first publication of note. Her collaborator, the "clever young Boston architect," as Mrs. Wharton once called him, was Ogden Codman, Jr. Although his fame in his own profession was long eclipsed by hers as a writer, it was largely through Codman that Mrs. Wharton formed the taste expressed first in this book and then, continually, in her subsequent novels commenting on high society and its habitat. "Edith Wharton was reacting against the social and intellectual desert of her 'good' family background in New York," observed an English critic nearly a hundred years later, "Codman was advocating the values of his New England childhood, both were flinching from the vulgarity of much modern American life."[1]

Published in New York in 1897, *The Decoration of Houses* is certainly the most influential work on interior decoration in modern times and can be considered the genesis of the look we call Manhattan Style today. In it Codman and Mrs. Wharton sought to resurrect the principles of classic design, extolling *simplicity, symmetry,* and *suitability* as the ultimate criteria of good taste, and asserting the importance of integrating the interior decoration of a room with its basic architecture.

It was a premise that was to recur, as we shall see, in the credo of every designer who has influenced design, Manhattan-style, throughout the ensuing century. At the time the book appeared, however, the authors could assert that "No study of *house-decoration as a branch of architecture* has for at least fifty years been published in England or America," although, as they went on to point out, "France is always producing admirable monographs on isolated branches of this subject."

In America (and England) in the 1890s, Victoriana was still flourishing; Codman and Wharton called the style "house decoration as *superficial application of ornament.*" The nouveaux riches — and there were many of them in those pre–income tax days — defined *culture* in terms of European architecture, art, and furniture, translated into houses that were overweeningly grand and choked with paintings, sculpture, and *objets d'art,* most of it imported from Europe. (Indeed, the American appetite for French art had grown so insatiable that the French government ordered an investigation in 1886 and then set about buying back its own.)[2]

Even the average home decorator of the day abhorred a void, it seemed. Pianos wore Spanish shawls; bouillon fringe streamed from every tufted, carved sofa; walls were dressed in ensembles of papers and hung with frame-to-frame artworks; sentimental memorabilia covered every available surface.

It was onto such a scene that *The Decoration of Houses* was launched. The authors wasted no time in establishing their premise; in the introduction to the book, they wrote:

> Rooms may be decorated in two ways: by a superficial application of ornament totally independent of structure, or by means of those architectural features which are part of the organism of every house, inside as well as out.

The book — still in print, and enjoying a revival as appreciation grows for Codman's work, especially — goes on to lay down a number of observations and dicta:

> Proportion is the good breeding of architecture.

> Architects are turning anew to the lost tradition of symmetry.

> The vulgarity of current decoration has its

source in the indifference of the wealthy to architectural fitness.

Patricians that they were, Codman and Wharton were confident that if good design were only practiced by the wealthy, it would "trickle down" to the masses.

Yet there is also a democratic voice to be heard in these pages — Mrs. Wharton's, no doubt, considering Codman's fabled disregard for money (even she hired another architect for The Mount, her most important house, saying that Codman had become too expensive):

> If little can be spent in buying furniture, willow arm-chairs (not rattan, as the models are too bad) with denim or corduroy will be more satisfactory than the "parlor suit" turned out in thousands by the manufacturer of cheap furniture, or the pseudo-Georgian or pseudo-Empire of the dealer in "high-grade goods."

Together they spoke out against the "ugliness of current designs" in furniture; against an "Athenian thirst for novelty [in styles] not always regulated by an Athenian sense of fitness"; against a "multiplicity of colors [which] always produces the same effect as a number of voices talking at the same time"; and against the prevailing craze for knickknacks: "Their absence improves even bad rooms, or makes them at least less multitudinously bad."

But Codman's and Mrs. Wharton's were not the only voices raised against the design excesses of the era. Nearing the turn of the century, the "American Renaissance" was in full swing, sending American painters, sculptors, and architects abroad for training at such schools as the Ecole des Beaux-Arts. The influential Charles Follen McKim, of McKim, Mead and White, had been urging architects to study and "understand the splendid standards of Classic and Renaissance art."[3] The much-publicized World's Columbian Exposition of 1893 in Chicago had celebrated monumental classical planning, art, and architecture in its famed "White City" of buildings. Looking back almost a century later, William Coles, the president of Classical America, described the Exposition's objective: it was to be "a great concert of the arts, collaborating under the guidance of architecture to submerge idiosyncrasy in the realization of a noble ideal." It succeeded, Coles said, in introducing classic ideals to Americans "on a vast and heroic scale."[4]

That winds of change had already begun to blow through the brown, gloomy interiors of the time was readily acknowledged in *The Decoration of Houses*. The book opens with the authors' observation that

> The last ten years have been marked by a notable development in architecture and decoration, and while France will long retain her present superiority in these arts, our own advance is perhaps more significant than that of any other country.

Even as Codman and Mrs. Wharton were hammering their manifesto into shape for their publisher, such "advances" were imminent at a certain Manhattan townhouse on Irving Place near fashionable Gramercy Park. Elsie de Wolfe, an actress whose main acclaim came from her costumes (she always wore the latest in French couture), had moved there in 1892 with her great friend Elisabeth Marbury. "The Bachelors," as they were called (not altogether flatteringly), quickly created an American salon, hostessing a series of Sunday-afternoon gatherings that glittered with some of the most social names and most interesting talents of the times. From New York and abroad came the likes of Ethel Barrymore, Nellie Melba, Stanford White (who was a neighbor), Oscar Wilde, Mrs. J. P. Morgan, and the Hewitt sisters, Sarah and Eleanor, daughters of the philanthropist Peter Cooper and future founders of what was to become the Smithsonian Institution's Museum of Decorative Arts in New York.

They flocked to the Irving house parties to lean an elbow on the ladies' mantelpiece or chair-arm and enjoy a lively discussion of the world, most especially the world of the arts. And if their art happened to be the theater, there might be business talk as well: Bessie Marbury had established herself as a theatrical agent and was on her way to becoming hugely successful, as perhaps the first woman in the field.

With her own theatrical career merely lukewarm — and cooling with age — Elsie de Wolfe was poised to create another kind of *first*. It is easy to imagine her in the increasingly long intervals between roles, a small, bright-eyed woman reclining deep among the multipatterned pillows and fern jungle of the house's then-fashionable "Turkish cozy corner." She would be deep in thought, too, no doubt remembering other, very different rooms, rooms fresh with light colors and freed of bric-a-brac, rooms where silken curtains whispered at the windows and the furniture was as comfortable as it was elegant.

She and Bessie had often visited such rooms. As their friendship — and Bessie's business — had grown, the two women had spent long sojourns in France. The friends they made and visited there, both expatriate Americans and French, included connoisseurs who had already come to appreciate the light, open airiness of eighteenth-century French decor. (Many Frenchmen did not agree, equating the style with life before the Revolution, barely a century in the past.)

At first Elsie just brought back an occasional piece of furniture from the period. Then she went after its very essence. Sometime between the fall of 1897 and the end of the next year, she completely transformed the house on Irving Place, clearing out the dark, ponderous furniture, lightening and purifying backgrounds, and banishing most of the bric-a-brac. She pulled up the layers of Turkish carpets, got rid of all the ferns and — most prophetic of all — painted both furniture and woodwork white, and hung a number of large mirrors, which were seldom seen in Victorian rooms but were very much in the eighteenth-century idiom.

The change astounded and delighted "the Bachelors'" social circle and made Elsie a leading lady after all. The stardom that she never accomplished on stage, she found in decorating. In creating a new role for herself, she invented an entirely new industry, going on to become America's first professional woman designer.

But there was another reason for Elsie de Wolfe's lasting impact: she established decorating as a *business*. Before her, people made do with an upholsterer, a curtain-maker, and their own inspiration. Elsie was a businesswoman who, as Diana Vreeland put it, "wasn't playing any games about being the clever little woman. . . . [She] was the first woman that any man would have sat and talked to in the million-dollar range."[5]

The male decorators who followed Elsie's lead also acknowledged her seminal role. As Billy Baldwin said years later,

> What Elsie did became the foundation for all that was to follow: she purged those Victorian houses of their stuffiness and clutter, got rid of the bad pictures and the bad furniture, began painting walls white, introduced the cult of the antique and the idea of comfort. Many of her ideas were imported straight from France and England.[6]

No one knows, of course, how many of Elsie's ideas also came from *The Decoration of Houses*. The book was published on December 3, 1897; by then the transformation of the Irving Place house seems to have been already under way. Certainly Elsie and Bessie had been to France and England many times before then, and Elsie's role as a tastemaker — at least in apparel fashions — is well documented in the media of the times. Elsie herself seems never to have so much as mentioned *The Decoration of Houses*, nor its authors, though she and Ogden Codman were later to collaborate on a number of projects, including architectural work on the Irving Place house. Together they also took on the highly publicized renovation of a brownstone on East Seventy-first Street that she bought in 1910 for a professional experiment. The project — a dramatic makeover of a typically stodgy rowhouse into a classically elegant and *very New York* town house — brought both of them fame and a flood of commissions, some of which they worked on together. Even later, when she bought another brownstone on East Fifty-fifth Street, this one to be home to her and Bessie, Elsie cheerfully set about duplicating all the architectural renovations Codman had shown her.[7] Then she went on to add touches that were distinctly her own, plus a number that were originally inspired by Codman but were soon to become *her* trademarks.

The use of treillage — then meant only for gardens — and that of chintz — then seen fit only for country living — are two outstanding examples of Codman innovations that came to flower in Elsie's hands. In 1905, when Stanford White recommended her to handle the interior decorating of the Colony Club, which he had designed, she surprised the haute monde members of this, the first American social club for women only, by filling it with humble glazed-cotton chintz and by bringing green-painted garden trellises *indoors* for the tearoom on the main floor. Codman, it is important to note, had used trellises in the resort houses he had designed in Newport, including Edith Wharton's own Land's End (their first collaboration). He had also championed chintz and toile de Jouy at least a decade earlier when he did over The Grange, his elegant early-eighteenth-century ancestral home in Lincoln, Massachusetts.

Codman's inspiration was also manifest in Elsie's largest and most important commission, the job that made her both world-famous and rich enough to truly afford the house she and Bessie had bought earlier in Versailles, France, the Villa Trianon. In 1913 Elsie persuaded Henry Clay Frick, the most important art collector in America, to let her design and buy the furnishings for the family's private rooms on the second floor of his Fifth Avenue residence. Along with the extraordinary French antiques she bought for the mansion, which is now open to the public as the Frick Collection, Elsie commissioned Alden Twachtman, son of the American Impressionist artist John H. Twachtman, to paint the ceilings in two corridors upstairs. The chinoiserie designs that she gave him to follow — monkeys cavorting against a soft blue sky — could have come straight from the ceiling of the château of Chantilly, painted in the Louis XV period. *Or they could have come from The Decoration of Houses*: Codman had used a photograph of the château's painting in the book to illustrate their chapter on ceilings and floors. For her version, Elsie was quick to grasp the potential of the new medium — electricity — and used it to illuminate the ceilings at the Frick mansion.

A century later, however, the exact provenance of ideas is less interesting than the *effect* of those ideas. A new taste in interiors was evolving, an approach to decorating that was lighter, more comfortable, and more "suitable" — and it was evolving in *New York City*.

Elsie de Wolfe (later Lady Mendl, after her surprise marriage, in 1926, to Sir Charles Mendl of the British embassy in Paris), did indeed influence succeeding generations of home decorators in America. Many were ordinary homemakers who read and emulated the advice she dispensed through her widely read columns in the *Delineator*, a popular women's magazine of the time, and through a book of her own, *The House in Good Taste* (1913); others were to follow directly through the door she had opened, taking up decorating as a profession. Ruby Ross Wood did both.

No less a literary light than Theodore Dreiser can take partial credit, at least, for the evolution of interior decorating into a legitimate profession. The first decade of the twentieth century found him in the editor's chair at the *Delineator*, commissioning, among other things, a series of articles on home decoration. Elsie de Wolfe agreed to supply ideas for the series but, since she was no writer herself, asked for a "ghost." Dreiser recruited a young woman from Georgia, an editor who had worked for a Hearst farm journal before moving on to writing free-lance articles. Ruby Ross Goodnow — later to become Ruby Ross Wood — could write but, as she protested to Dreiser, knew absolutely nothing about interior decoration. Dreiser prevailed. And by the time she had written those columns under Elsie's name, answered her reader mail, and gone on to ghost-write *The House in Good Taste*, Ruby Ross Wood was ready to take up a new career.

She did not put down her pen, however. Once out of Elsie's shadow, Mrs. Wood wrote a decorating book under her own name, called *The Honest House*, and published it in 1914. The same year, she joined the staff of Wanamaker's department store in Philadelphia. Wanamaker's in New York, meanwhile, was about to make design history: under the direction of another talented woman,

When the architect Stanford White recommended Elsie de Wolfe to decorate the Colony Club in 1905, her career as a decorator was launched. She surprised the society-women members by bringing garden trelliswork indoors, an idea inspired by Ogden Codman, Jr. (Photograph from Elsie de Wolfe, *The House in Good Taste*)

Nancy Vincent McClelland, it opened Au Quatrième, the first department in the world devoted entirely to antiques and home decorating. Four years later, when Nancy McClelland left to go out on her own, Ruby Ross Wood became Au Quatrième's director. But the future, as seen through her famous tinted glasses, looked rosy indeed for independent decorators, and by the 1920s Ruby Ross Wood, Inc., was out there competing with her old mentor, Elsie de Wolfe.

There was ample room for them both in the postwar economic boom. In fact, for a profession that was a scant two decades old, the decorating field was getting downright crowded. And while Paris was teeming with creative genius that would exert great influence on America, New York was in the forefront of the home front. A major factor in the city's growing eminence was the Parsons School of Design. That was not yet its name, however. Founded by William Merritt Chase in 1896 to teach painting, the New York School of Fine and Applied Arts had begun as early as 1904 to offer courses in interior decoration. By then Frank Alvah Parsons had joined the faculty, first as a teacher who was to help chart the history of interior design, then as the school's innovative president, until his death, in 1930. Ten years later, the school was renamed in Parsons's honor.

He had come to teach, armed with a bachelor's degree in science, and quickly applied a "scientific" approach to the study of interior design. No one would have been more pleased than the authors of *The Decoration of Houses,* who had spoken out against the "confusion resulting from . . . unscientific methods [of] piling up heterogeneous ornament." Codman and Mrs. Wharton had called for "mathematical calculation" and "scientific adjustment of voids and masses" to produce the proportions they referred to as "good breeding in architecture."[8] Codman's own designs were the result of meticulous study and exacting measurement of specific architectural sources, and the book supported the thesis that there are laws of good taste that never vary, that always govern the proportion of rooms and the design of furniture. In the parlance of the nineteenth century, they were preaching scientific eclecticism.

The New York School practiced it. By 1913, the year Frank Alvah Parsons became its president, the school could proclaim in its catalog, " 'Interior decoration' " — the quotes are in the original — "like architecture, has reached the dignity of a profession." Rather than receiving instruction in simple drawing and color, students learned to draw elevations; they were taught the history of art in terms of "periods" and studied constructive

Ruby Ross Wood's sure hand with classic furnishings — and unconventional color schemes — distinguishes this study/morning room, done sometime before 1920. The walls are pale-pink faux marble, with painted lapis lazuli, malachite, black, and touches of gold. (Photograph from *House & Garden's Book of Interiors*)

and decorative architecture. Parsons himself pulled together the school's objectives in the book he wrote in 1915, *Interior Decoration: Its Principles and Practice*. And at about the same time, obviously acknowledging the birth of decorating as a *business,* the school instituted studies in materials, focusing on textiles, rugs, carpets, and wallpapers, with problems given on cost estimating and "connections made with the trade for the sale of same."

Most innovative and influential of all were the school-sponsored trips abroad, offering advanced study of the historical periods "in their natural environment"—Europe. Beginning in 1915–1916, these study trips were led by Parsons and a young graduate of the school, William Odom, class of '08, who had returned in short order to teach there. Six years or so later Odom headed the Department of Interior Architecture and Decoration, and it was his determined emphasis on architecture that was to give the school — and the students it trained — such enormous influence on interior design over the next half century.

Odom knew his subject matter intimately. A native of Georgia, he had come to New York to study painting under William Merritt Chase (and music with Leopold Stokowski, as well), but his interest in architecture and design had led him to the New York School, and then to Paris and the Ecole des Beaux-Arts. His travels and study in France and Italy convinced him that seeing was learning; by 1920 he had in turn convinced Parsons to open a Paris branch of the school. *Arbiter elegantiae* that Odom was, he soon located on the Place des Vosges, in an elegant seventeenth-century house filled with splendid *boiserie* and fine French furniture from Louis XIV through the Empire. Odom, who was justifiably dubbed "Mr. Taste," is remembered as distant and glacial, a teacher who communicated largely through intermediate instructors but who nonetheless exerted a profound influence on both his students and the design profession in general, especially as Parsons disciples began to come back from Paris to practice in New York.

Odom lived what he taught — the school itself was an architectural treasure, and the furnishings within were "discreetly grand" and arranged, it is said, according to Odom's "fanatical respect for symmetry." It was, however, for the field trips that the students were there, and Odom, with his unimpeachable social connections, was uniquely equipped to lead them. Throughout France and Italy they went, with measuring rods and notebooks in hand, into the most important buildings — both public *and* private, thanks to Odom's en-

The Parisian drawing room that was to influence generations of New York designers: Jean-Michel Frank's spare, rigidly edited design for the Vicomte and Vicomtesse de Noailles, done in the early 1930s, focused on lush finishes, as seen in the vellum parchment wall covering and the straw-marquetry screens. An early version of the Parsons table appears at left. (Photograph courtesy *House & Garden*)

trée. There was one three-month course offered in England (in 1923), but the focus remained on France and Italy. Odom, it seems, had little interest in English design. For that matter, neither Codman nor Mrs. Wharton nor Elsie de Wolfe ever paid much attention to English or American decorative arts. Having grown up with the genre, each found new inspiration in France and Italy.

Named president of Parsons in 1930, Odom moved back and forth between both schools, Paris and New York, and died in New York in 1942. He was buried, at his own request, in London. But he left Parsons in the capable hands of — even "willed it" to, some said — a younger protégé, Van Day Truex. Kansas-born, with a disarming twang, Truex was as open as Odom had been austere, and every bit as elegant in his own way. He had arrived as a student at Parsons, Paris, in 1925, to find a "traffic jam . . . of creative talent." Paris was a "snobbish world," he later wrote, "but it was a snobbery of talent and spirit" in which Truex said he "wandered, mesmerized, for fifteen years."[9]

One of the talents he found so mesmerizing was a young designer named Jean-Michel Frank. Although he had been educated in law, Frank was also interested in the simple, spare furniture of the late Louis XVI period. While Art Deco raged all around him, he remained intent on creating severe, intellectual designs that distilled furniture to its very essence. Frank's rooms were almost surrealistically empty; the sight of one of his interiors led Jean Cocteau to make his famous quip, "Pity the burglars got everything."[10] But Frank's designs also boasted exquisite finishes in rare and luxurious materials: shagreen and varnished straw marquetry, vellum, macassar ebony, glittering squares of gypsum mica. Conversely, he would create surprises by covering Louis XVI armchairs in cowhide or men's suiting. And he liked to juxtapose the elegant and the Peasant in the rooms he created for his international set of clients.

Frank's inspirations came from many sources — ancient Greece, Rome, Egypt, the Surrealist movement then at play in Paris — and the artists who translated them into furnishings for the shop he opened with Adolphe Chanaux included legendary names: Salvador Dali; the Giacometti brothers, Alberto and Diego; Emilio Terry, another important interior decorator, and Christian Bérard, the painter, fashion illustrator, and designer of costumes and theater sets.

Van Day Truex was not alone in his excitement over the work flowing from the Frank-Chanaux ateliers. From the moment the shop opened its doors in 1932, such New York designers as Elsie

Syrie Maugham, an admirer of Jean-Michel Frank, built this early 1930s dining room around a number of works from his shop in Paris. The consoles, trees, and chimneypiece are by Serge Roché; Giacometti made the lamps, and Frank himself designed the bench. (Photograph courtesy Millar & Harris, 1935)

de Wolfe, Syrie Maugham, and Eleanor Brown bought pieces eagerly for clients back in America. Frank himself created Nelson Rockefeller's living room in New York (with Wallace Harrison, in 1937). His minimalist approach continues to influence new generations of New York designers, and at least one of his ideas has proliferated throughout the world — the simple T-square, or Parsons, table that evolved from his lectures at the Paris school.

"The students in the department of interior design were fascinated by him," Van Day Truex recalled, and before long "his designs for tables and consoles of severe Chinese influence began to appear in their contemporary rooms."[11]

A friend as well as an admirer of Frank's talent, Truex stepped in at the beginning of World War II and helped to arrange backing by McMillen, Incorporated, so Frank could continue his work in New York. It was not to happen. A melancholy, sensitive man with a tragic family life, Frank came to New York in 1941, but within a week he was dead by his own hand.

By contrast, life for Van Day Truex was a series of continuing triumphs. A born teacher, he influenced generations of students between 1942, when he took over as the president of Parsons, and 1953, when the school abruptly changed direction. With his admonitions to "control, edit, and distill!" ringing in their ears, Truex's students learned historical accuracy, drawing, and experimentation.[12] He made interior decorating both a serious business and an exciting one.

In his next career, Truex was equally influential. Two years after leaving Parsons, he was hired by Walter Hoving to be design director of Tiffany & Company. He set the store — which Billy Baldwin characterized at the time as "stuffy, boring, old-fashioned, middle-class, and impossible"[13] — on a new and newsworthy course. In the tradition of Jean-Michel Frank with his ateliers, Truex brought major design talents to bear on the silver, glass, and china offered by the store. His own design for a Baccarat crystal decanter shaped like a Bordeaux bottle, nicknamed "Van ordinaire," is now in the collection of the Museum of Modern Art. And his celebrated bamboo silverware pattern is still among Tiffany's best-sellers.

For all his success in New York, however, Van Day Truex remained mesmerized by France. In fact, he was making plans to buy the first home he had ever owned in America when a heart attack felled him in 1979.

Meanwhile, back in New York, interior decorating as a *profession* was gaining momentum and a new corps of practitioners. Although the Parsons School would soon be turn-

ing out trained, disciplined decorators, many of those already at work in the 1920s were women for whom the right social credentials were enough. They may have been unschooled, but always they were instinctively *knowing* in matters of taste, style, and "suitability." Elsie de Wolfe, who could have trademarked the very word *suitability*, was still very much on the scene, though by now she divided her time between her villa in Versailles and New York. By now, too, she was wearing a Legion d'Honneur medal, awarded for service as a nurse during World War I, and had taken to standing on her head for exercise and tinting her gray hair pale blue.

They were a colorful lot, these first women in decorating, which only enhanced the allure of the profession for those to follow. Ruby Ross Wood favored simple dresses in black with a bright scarf always at her throat, wore pink-tinted tortoise-shell glasses, and had become known for her fresh color and her arrangement of "beautiful things comfortably." Mrs. Wood made another important contribution to the development of design in New York: she hired a dapper young man from Baltimore named Billy Baldwin, about whom we will hear more later.

And there was also the Australian-born Rose Cumming, who grew up on a sheep farm, got into decorating rather by accident, and was audacious in her use of color — even that of her own hair, which she tinted violet. Rose Cumming's rooms were pure exoticism. She silvered walls in foil wrapping paper, hung smoked mirrors and billowing curtains of the vivid chintzes that became her trademark, and stood an eclectic mix of traditional furniture on bare, highly polished parquet floors. She paid no mind to authenticity: any period would do, "as long as the furnishings were old and beautiful, romantic and lush, exotic and original."[14] Her eccentricities were born of natural "flair," uninhibited by the kind of disciplined study going on at the New York School. The story goes that young Rose came to New York en route to join her fiancé in England. England was at war, and since America was still neutral in 1917, she was hoping — in vain, as it turned out — to book passage from the States. Stuck in New York, Miss Cumming decided to stay and get a job. When Frank Crowninshield, then the editor of *Vanity Fair*, suggested that she become a decorator, her celebrated reply was, "What is it?"

She soon found out, making a brief landing at Au Quatrième and then moving on — by mutual consent, it is said — to open her own shop on Madison Avenue and fill it with a virtual bewilderment of antiques, flowers, and fabrics. Her shop windows became a must-see; everyone, including the press, came running when they were changed. The fabrics — silks and chintzes that she had colored to her taste — are still legendary, and some are still available.

Literally less colorful but nonetheless equally influential on New York taste were the all-white rooms of the London-born Syrie Maugham, who opened her famed Fifty-seventh Street shop in the late 1920s. Née Gwendoline Maude Syrie Barnardo and married to the author Somerset Maugham, she "caught the 'no colour' virus and spread the disease around the world. . . . For the next decade Syrie Maugham bleached, pickled, or scraped every piece of furniture in sight."[15] She stripped and pickled walls, moulding, and paneling. She sewed sheepskins together to make carpets, introduced white plaster lamps and furniture from the Paris shop of Jean-Michel Frank and Adolphe Chanaux, and was to make her trade-mark flower, the calla lily, *the* symbol of the thirties.

Despite Elsie de Wolfe's warning to Syrie that "the decorating field is already overcrowded," that crowd was soon to include another singular talent, Dorothy Tuckerman Draper. Born into the elite clique in Tuxedo Park, New York — she liked to say that she had "escaped through a hole in the fence" — and married to Dr. George Draper, she may have started out as a "society-lady decorator," but Dorothy Draper had bigger ideas. She became the first woman in America to specialize in nonresidential design. Hotel and apartment lobbies all over New York soon bloomed with the Dorothy Draper look: giant cabbage roses were her signature, as were overscaled black-and-white-checked floors, large ornamental appliqués in white plaster, and a zest for mixing furniture of various periods without a nod to provenance.

Jean-Michel Frank and the architect Wallace Harrison designed the living room of the Nelson Rockefellers' New York apartment in 1937. Pictured are an overmantel painting by Matisse, a rug by Christian Bérard, and chairs and a table by Frank himself. (Photograph courtesy Mrs. Nelson A. Rockefeller)

A large, imperious figure herself ("She reminded me of a gladiator," said her successor, Carleton Varney), Dorothy Draper wore hats that made her loom even larger — one reason, perhaps, that she also favored giant lamps with extroverted shades and room schemes on such a sweeping scale. She hated seeing small, personal objects in a room; she loved bold gestures, such as slicking an entire row of Sutton Place houses in black paint and then adding white trim and a rainbow of doors, each a different color. Billy Baldwin, who once lived in one of these houses, said Dorothy Draper should be "eternally thanked"[16] for her bravery.

Other design historians since have called the Draper style neobaroque and even Surrealistic, but her ebullient version of Manhattan Style had a universal appeal. Soon her influence was reflected in hotels and homes across the country, the latter largely through the disarming "you-can-do-it, too" columns she wrote as director of *Good Housekeeping* magazine's Studio of Living and in newspapers nationwide.

New York society also nurtured another young woman who entered the decorating field in the 1920s. Eleanor Stockstrom McMillen was not, however, "one of the ladies,"[17] as she once told an interviewer. Married to an engineer, Drury McMillen (and later to the architect Archibald Brown), she spent three years at the New York School of Fine and Applied Arts and then went to Paris to study with William Odom. It was "a privilege to have an education under Mr. Odom and Mr. Parsons," Eleanor Brown, then a trustee of the school, was to observe years later. Indeed, Mrs. Brown set such store by the teaching process at Parsons that over the next forty years her firm hired only one staff member who was not a Parsons graduate.

Odom was McMillen's mentor in more ways than one: it was he who initially encouraged her to open her own shop, and it was he who found and shipped over the fine-quality furniture and *objets,* mostly from the late eighteenth and early nineteenth centuries, that were to set the style for which McMillen would become known. Traditional, classic, certainly conservative, Mrs. Brown called her company "the first professional full-service interior decorating firm in America." Having studied business and gone to secretarial school, armed with a design degree, Mrs. Brown brought an added professionalism to an industry that often thrived on "flair." She developed a system for the complex paperwork and record-keeping that is still known as the McMillen Method, and she believed that good design started with the bones of a room, its architecture.

Never trendy, but also never stodgy or dated in its design approach, the firm has always been sought out by the wealthy, the powerful, and the influential, who appreciate its understated, "old-money" approach. Equally influential on the development of design, McMillen, Incorporated, has served as training ground for a number of more recent stars in the field, including Mark Hampton, Albert Hadley, and Kevin McNamara.

Eleanor Brown herself may have helped launch another important influence on decorating, Manhattan-style. In the late 1920s she decorated the Gracie Square house of Mr. and Mrs. Henry Parish II. He was a well-to-do banker; she was the nineteen-year-old Dorothy May Kinnicutt, nicknamed "Sister" by her four brothers. The oft-told story has it that as a new bride honeymooning in Paris, Sister announced, "I'm going to be a decorator, just like Elsie de Wolfe." Whether the inspiration was Eleanor Brown or Elsie, the impetus was the Depression. When the going got tough for her husband, Sister Parish got going "to make both ends meet." Her early practice among friends in affluent Far Hills, New Jersey, grew dramatically after she opened a shop on Madison Avenue in New York. In the style of the early grandes dames of decorating, Sister Parish was untutored, though not uneducated. After graduating with the horsey upper crust from Foxcroft, she had traveled widely, seen the great houses both here and abroad, and known what she was looking at. More important, she also knew what others of her ilk were looking *for*: rooms that bespoke heritage and breeding but said it softly, with the confidence born of good background. The "English Manor House Look" comes close to summing up her style, but there is more to it than that, especially after Albert Hadley brought his contemporary point of view — and his name — to the firm in 1962.

The 1960s marked the high point of another career that still influences the direction of interior design — or, rather, of interior *decorating,* as Billy Baldwin persisted in calling it. After two years at Princeton, young Baldwin was already decorating for clients in his native Baltimore when he met Ruby Ross Wood — whom he called "my goddess in a rumpled raincoat." He came to New York and joined her firm in 1935, creating his own office in the image that was to become a Baldwin trademark: the walls were a glossy dark brown, "the color that has haunted me all my life," as he was to write nearly forty years later. The furnishings were simple, understated, and *good*, also in the Baldwin idiom. And he saw *good* in the simplest fabrics and styles. Cotton became another Baldwin signature; he also followed Elsie de Wolfe's lead in liberating the little armless slipper chair from bedroom duty and used it to great effect in the up-front rooms of his clients. He designed a series of tubular brass bookcases for Cole Porter's New York apartment that are still regarded as classics. And he believed in mixing fine antiques with the very new.

What Baldwin had done was to express his own, highly personal interpretation of Manhattan Style. The tradition that started nearly a century ago with the high-minded ideals of Ogden Codman, Jr., and Edith Wharton has been reinterpreted through the decades by each generation of designers working in New York City. Always their visions of Manhattan Style have been highly individualistic; often their interpretations have reflected the ebb and flow of stylistic trends at work beyond the city itself. Modernism, Minimalism, Traditionalism, Neoclassicism — the prevailing influences of every era have appeared, peaked, and been assimilated into the look, even as the disciples of each have melded into New York's great legacy of design.

These names are legendary; the list is long. There was William Pahlmann, another product of the Parsons School, remembered for his colorfully eclectic model rooms at department stores such as Lord & Taylor during the 1930s and celebrated still for his landmark interiors in the Four Seasons restaurant. Carrying forward that tradition into the 1960s, Barbara D'Arcy made her room settings at Bloomingdale's into major events for design professionals, the admiring public, and the media. Equally newsworthy have been the works of such diverse talents as Donald Deskey, immortalized by his designs for Radio City Music Hall; the industrial designer Raymond Loewy; and Edward Wormley, a noted designer of furniture and interiors from the 1930s to the 1970s. Also beginning in the 1930s, Robsjohn-Gibbings — English-born, avant-garde, and outspoken — created furniture and rooms of spare elegance.

Manhattan-born Ward Bennett's name lives on in theater design as well as interiors; James Amster's survives in the East Forty-ninth Street courtyard that has become a New York City landmark. Many other names underscore New York's claim to being the design capital of America. Some are from the 1940s: Sarah Hunter Kelly, George Stacey, and Joseph Platt, whose interiors for *Gone with the Wind* were as vivid as the film itself. In the ensuing decades, Yale R. Burge, Melanie Kahane, Ellen Lehmann McCluskey, Emilie Malino, and Michael Greer added their own dimensions to the look we call Manhattan Style.

But though individual designers may change the details, the look itself remains distinct.

Stanley Barrows, himself a graduate of and former teacher at Parsons who is known as "The Professor" to generations of later Parsons students, ventured to define the look: "It's a degree of sophistication, taste, and experience practiced by New York designers that's just not found anywhere else. The city itself helps create it: New Yorkers see so much. . . . They have so much choice. . . . There's so much going on: the art, the auction houses, the extraordinary antique shops, the general excitement of all the activity in town. New York designers develop a knowing eye.

"A knowing eye — that's how I'd define Manhattan Style." ☐

A gathering of the early greats at an Amster Yard party in the late 1930s. *From left*: James Amster, Marian Hall, Ruby Ross Wood (in armchair), Billy Baldwin, William Pahlmann, Dorothy Draper (wearing hat), and Nancy McClelland. (Photograph, private collection)

"Order, for the sake of harmony, and in the hope of beauty"

OGDEN CODMAN, JR.

Those words may have been Edith Wharton's, but it was Ogden Codman, Jr., who made them into the motto that governed his work throughout his long life (1863–1951).

Codman's formal training in architecture was scant; he spent a year at the Massachusetts Institute of Technology — an unhappy year, by all accounts — and then got down to actual practice with several architectural firms in his native Boston. But Codman's feeling for elegant, classical forms and understated interior decoration was innate, as instinctive as the celebrated snobbery that would, years later, lead him to reject even the Duke and Duchess of Windsor as tenants at his beloved La Leopolda, the villa he designed for himself on the French Riviera.

"I am sorry," he reportedly said to the disappointed Duke after their negotiations over rental terms fell through, "that the House of Codman cannot do business with the House of Windsor."

The "House of Codman" had beginnings auspicious enough to inspire such imperiousness: born to a prominent Boston family, young Ogden was raised on his grandfather's classic eighteenth-century estate in Lincoln, Massachusetts. Then, when he was nine years old, the family moved to France for a decade. There he developed the passion for French classicism that was to be the other great influence on his work.

Once he was back in America, Codman set about measuring and drawing many of Boston's fine old buildings, especially those by Charles Bulfinch, one American architect whose work he seems to have admired. Much of this was done under the direction of his uncle John Hubbard Sturgis, an architect who once designed an "incurably ugly" Stick Style Victorian house not far from Newport, Rhode Island. When the Theodore Whartons bought the house, named Land's End, in 1892, it marked the beginning of a series of events that was to profoundly affect the course of interior design for at least a century to come. She, of course, was the Mrs. Wharton with whom Codman would publish *The Decoration of Houses* five

years later. The couple hired the "clever young architect from Boston" to cure the "incurably ugly" house, and in working together, Puss, as he called her, and Coddy, as she called him, discovered their mutual taste for simplified architecture and uncluttered, lightened rooms.

The work on Land's End lasted several years, during which, as Mrs. Wharton wrote later, they "drifted, I hardly know how, toward the notion of putting [their ideas] into a book."

That book helped to transform the gloom and jumble of Victoriana into clean, open, comfortable rooms. And Edith Wharton was to help Codman's own career dramatically by introducing him to the likes of Cornelius Vanderbilt, for whom he designed the upper floors at The Breakers in Newport. It was in New York, however, that Codman did his most influential work. Many of his ideas would be adopted and popularized by Elsie de Wolfe and disseminated into the mainstream of interior design through the teachings of the New York School of Fine and Applied Arts.

Codman was a great patron of the school (along with Elsie de Wolfe, Edith Wharton, and Walter Gay, the artist whose paintings affectionately recorded many of the era's most splendid rooms).

One of the last commissions Codman carried out in New York was the Archer Huntington town house at 1083 Fifth Avenue. Completed in 1917, before Codman gave in completely to the lure of his beloved France, the house remains as elegant testimony to the beliefs with which Codman and Mrs. Wharton brought their seminal book to its conclusion:

> The supreme excellence is simplicity. Moderation, fitness, relevance — these are the qualities that give permanence. . . . There is no absolute perfection, there is no communicable ideal; but much that is empiric, much that is confused and extravagant, will give way before the application of principles based on common sense and regulated by the laws of harmony and proportion. □

The vast library of Codman's own East Ninety-sixth Street house featured a rug with Robert Adam—inspired garlands set against a foliated background. Over the central motif is a Louis XV chandelier. Codman amassed an enormous library, much of it devoted to classic design in New England and France. (Photograph courtesy the Metropolitan Museum of Art, Gift of the Estate of Ogden Codman, Jr., 1951)

Right: In typical neoclassic style, Codman used black and white marble on the entry floor of the house that he designed for himself at 7 East Ninety-sixth Street. A mirrored door created the additional window he needed to ensure symmetry and continue the progression of arches down the hall to the dining room.

Below: A Codman trademark, the oval dining room of the same house is centered with the kind of diminished-coffers motif often found in reverse in the domes of neoclassic buildings. The marble figures in the niche and the screen are both Louis XVI; the console and chandelier are Louis XV. (Photographs courtesy the Metropolitan Museum of Art, Gift of the Estate of Ogden Codman, Jr., 1951 and 1964)

Left: Edith Wharton's own sitting room attests to the ease with which Codman could use classical proportions on an intimate scale. Louis XVI chairs, upholstered to match the red-striped wallpaper, are drawn up to the late Louis XV *bibliothèque;* the grisaille corner cabinet stands next to an oval-backed Louis XVI chair.

Below: The dining room of the house at 884 Park Avenue, as designed by Ogden Codman for — and with — Edith Wharton after her divorce, in 1911, featured hand-blocked wallpaper with a late-eighteenth-century French design. The large Italian mirror was painted and gilded. The commodes were French; the chairs, reproductions in a simplified Empire style.
(Photographs courtesy the Metropolitan Museum of Art, Gift of the Estate of Ogden Codman, Jr., 1951)

"Suitability, simplicity, and proportion"

ELSIE de WOLFE

The scene is easy to picture: Elsie de Wolfe, grande dame of this new business of interior decorating, is propped among her pillows and poodles, receiving a visitor in her bedroom. The guest is Syrie Maugham, estranged from her author husband, Somerset Maugham, and contemplating a new career. Should she open a decorating shop, Syrie asks the woman who "invented" the business.

"You're too late, my dear, much too late," came Elsie's oft-quoted opinion. "The decorating field is already overcrowded."

The fact that Syrie opted to join the crowd anyway didn't bother the unflappable Elsie de Wolfe. Jane S. Smith, her biographer, reports that Elsie would even go on shopping expeditions with her new competitor, who quickly picked up the de Wolfe fondness for white and turned it into her own trademark. No matter to Elsie. By then she was off in new directions of her own, always a trailblazer with complete confidence in her taste and ideas.

It was a confidence shared by some of the most monied and influential people of her era, on both sides of the Atlantic. The de Wolfe style — light, elegant, comfortable, and committed to the neoclassic tradition — was a fresh breeze blowing into the dark, cluttered rooms of the late nineteenth century. If her look was derivative of eighteenth-century France, if it embodied many of the ideas set forth earlier by Ogden Codman, Jr., and Edith Wharton in *The Decoration of Houses*, it quickly became pure Elsie. Codman and Wharton wrote to admonish and enlighten the wealthy; Elsie translated good taste into concepts for everyman's home. Not that Elsie ever worked in humble surroundings herself — her clients included the likes of Fricks, Vanderbilts, and Morgans —

Right: When her friend Bessie Marbury moved to the previously unfashionable area known as Sutton Place, Elsie de Wolfe decorated her house, blending eighteenth-century Chinese wallpaper with the "serious" Georgian paneling of the second-floor sitting room.

Below: The leopard prints that would become a de Wolfe trademark here cover Louis XV side chairs and hassock. The window treatment and the eighteenth-century folding porcelain screen enhance the Chinese spirit of the room. (Photographs courtesy the New-York Historical Society, Mattie Edwards Hewitt Collection)

but she made her ideas, at least, accessible and popular. As the design historian C. Ray Smith observed, "Despite the stylistic changes of the past half century, the tradition that Elsie de Wolfe established in both her work and her writing about it persists as the foundation of American interior decorating in the late twentieth century."

Central to that tradition — and initially so shocking to the nineteenth-century eye — was the palette of light colors and neutral tones that Elsie favored: ivory, light gray, pale blues and roses, white, and beige, especially beige. A favorite de Wolfe anecdote — and there are many about this wry and witty woman — concerns her first trip to the Parthenon. "It's beige," she exclaimed. "Just my color!"

Elsie also reintroduced mirrors and mirrored walls, an eighteenth-century delight that had been little used in the nineteenth century. She mixed furniture periods and styles with a free hand, felt no compunction about putting reproductions alongside rare antiques, and eschewed elaborate fabrics in favor of simple chintzes. Writing in *The House in Good Taste*, she related cheerfully:

> When I began my work as a decorator of houses, my friends, astonished and just a little amused at my persistent use of chintz, called me the "Chintz decorator."

Whatever achieved the effect she was seeking was what Elsie used throughout her long career (beginning around the turn of the century and lasting to her death, in 1950). It could be said that she created the eclecticism that still characterizes interior design, Manhattan-style. Certainly she pioneered the use of contemporary art in traditional settings, and she never hesitated to introduce new and unexpected ingredients: plastic and glass, fur throws, leopard and zebra prints, and legions of small pillows embroidered with the witticisms of the international set. "Never Complain, Never Explain" was her favorite. Apparently Elsie herself did neither. It would not have been her style, and style was what she was all about, from her early years as an actress whose *clothes*, at least, brought rave reviews, to her final days at her beloved Villa Trianon in France. She even personally ordered the Cartier stationery that her husband, Sir Charles Mendl, would use to answer letters of condolence after her death. And just three weeks before that came, she played hostess to a party of visiting students from Parsons. Whether or not it was embroidered on one of her famous pillows, they — and generations of other decorators who followed in Elsie's footsteps — would carry forth her guidelines in the industry she founded: "Suitability, simplicity, and proportion." □

The treillage that had served Elsie so well at the Colony Club was repeated in the soaring ballroom of Bessie Marbury's house. The garden statuary, painted murals, and cane Louis XVI furniture all contributed to the alfresco atmosphere. (Photograph courtesy the New-York Historical Society, Mattie Edwards Hewitt Collection)

Right: World War II drove Elsie de Wolfe (by then Lady Mendl) from France to a suite at the St. Regis in New York. A number of her French and English antiques, including this Queen Anne secretary, came with her, as did the famous little pillow on the loveseat, proclaiming her motto, "Never complain, never explain."

Below: The suite was painted deep laurel green with white mouldings. Motto pillows on the ivory damask–covered sofa were red, blue, and green; the green fern-patterned fabric is still available a half century later. (Photographs courtesy *House & Garden*)

Left: Always open to anything new and interesting to her eye, Elsie incorporated Art Deco urns on glass pedestals, a plastic version of an Italian Empire bench, and unframed plate mirrors in the entry of Hope Hampton's house at 1145 Park Avenue.

Below: In the living room, Elsie gave Mrs. Hampton a spread of leopard print over wall-to-wall carpeting; a pair of Louis XV chairs face away from the mirror-framed Adam fireplace.(1935). (Photographs courtesy the New-York Historical Society, Mattie Edwards Hewitt Collection)

"Mr. Taste"

WILLIAM ODOM

Although his name is no longer familiar to the public, William Odom was enormously important to the development of interior design as a profession, greatly influencing both those decorators who charted its course in the early part of the century and the many who still practice his teachings today, a half century after his death.

It was Odom who recognized the importance of eighteenth-century French and Italian design at a time when many American collectors were still cramming their drawing rooms full of ponderous Victoriana. He believed that contemporary interior decoration must be grounded in an understanding of the past; accordingly, as head of the Paris branch of the Parsons School, he made it possible for American students to explore the crème of European classic design firsthand.

Later, when he became president of Parsons, Odom continued to feed the appetite he had helped to create among New York designers for quality antiques. The continuous supply of eighteenth- and early-nineteenth-century furniture that he shipped back from France gave such firms as McMillen, Incorporated, a leading edge in the increasingly competitive New York design business. That the hallmark of the elegant Manhattan room was to become, by midcentury, fine — often signed — French antiques, classically arranged within architecturally correct backgrounds, was due almost entirely to Odom's influence.

His sense of style was impeccable, and legendary. His sobriquet, "Mr. Taste," was apt. As Eleanor Brown once observed, William Odom "couldn't put a book down on a table in a way that didn't look special."

Opposite: In his apartment at the Pierre Hotel, photographed in the early 1930s, Odom ordered his collections with obsessive symmetry and characteristic formality. The lamps were made from Italian Empire candlesticks that show Egyptian influence. (Photograph courtesy *House & Garden*)

Connoisseurs flocked to the McMillen, Incorporated, town house in April 1946 for the sale of Odom's collections. Eleanor Brown arranged the furnishings with the precision she had learned as Odom's student in Paris. (Photograph courtesy McMillen, Incorporated)

In his Pierre Hotel apartment, Odom centered a contemporary mirror on the chimneypiece between a pair of Italian baroque mirrors. Crouching blackamoor sculptures support twin tables flanking the fireplace; the chairs are Louis XVI.
(Photograph courtesy *House & Garden)*

Opposite: By the late 1930s, Odom had replaced the Italian mirrors with English flower paintings from the mid–nineteenth century. His drawing room nonetheless retained its elegance and sense of timelessness.
(Photograph courtesy Stanley Barrows)

The word *ordinary* was not in Odom's vocabulary. He spent his whole life searching for the extraordinary. His scholarship was as unimpeachable as the social connections he employed to open the great houses of Europe to Parsons students. At age twenty he started work on a major two-volume study, *The History of Italian Furniture*, which was published in 1916 and reprinted fifty years later and is still considered the most authoritative book on the subject.

Odom's own collections, an eclectic ingathering of superb eighteenth- and early-nineteenth-century furniture and objects, were so fine that after his death part went to the Musée des Arts Decoratifs in Paris, while Yale University received his two-thousand-volume library on travel and art. The bulk of Odom's collection, however, passed into the hands of other connoisseurs via McMillen, Incorporated, and the famous exhibition and private sale staged there by Odom's admirer Eleanor Brown. She had her firm's townhouse on East Fifty-fifth Street repainted and arranged with Odom's furnishings for the sale, which helped raise funds for Parsons. That would have pleased Odom; so would the words of a critic of the day, commenting on the collection and the taste behind it in *House & Garden* magazine: "His legacy was a discrimination which raised the standard of decoration in our time."   □

"Marvelous taste . . .
and a sense of what is correct"

ELEANOR McMILLEN BROWN

S ocial Register" from its inception, the decorating firm founded in 1924 by Eleanor Stockstrom McMillen (later Brown) has steered a steady course through more than half a century of shifting fashions, fads, and societal changes. The company was a success from the moment Mrs. McMillen opened the doors of her town house on East Fifty-fifth Street, and it has never veered from the look its Parsons-trained founder established in doing the houses of her own social circle: traditional and elegant, yes, but also comfortable, livable, and so enduring that Betty Sherrill, today's president of McMillen, Incorporated, confides that she has not changed her own New York apartment in some twenty-five years.

The company itself is hardly given to change. Mrs. Sherrill has been with McMillen since her graduation, in 1951, from Parsons, where she was a student when Van Day Truex was president. In fact, that still makes her something of a new-comer: Eleanor Robertson Smith joined the firm in 1929 and remains active today. Another extraordinary talent, Grace Fakes, spent nearly forty years at McMillen, enhancing the company's reputation for understanding interior architecture and interpreting it for contemporary living.

"We *are* a bit old-fashioned here," Betty Sherrill concedes with a laugh.

Indeed, the operative word at McMillen today continues to be *we*. Ask Mrs. Sherrill to describe the "McMillen look," and she says, "*We're* eclectic. *We* draw on all sources — there's always a Venetian mirror and we always have a Chinese lacquer coffee table. We love lacquered desks, too, and painted furniture, and, of course, the Odom chairs."

William Odom was a great influence on Eleanor McMillen Brown, beginning with her student days

Eleanor Brown's own apartment confirms her belief that "the basic rules of proportion and scale never change": she may have the rooms painted every twenty years or so, and the fabrics replaced, but the color, the arrangement, and the furniture have all remained the same for fifty years. The Venetian red lacquer secretary has presided over Mrs. Brown's yellow and white living room since she moved into the apartment in 1928; it is now being reproduced as part of the McMillen Collection. (Photographs courtesy McMillen, Incorporated)

at the New York School of Fine and Applied Arts (later called the Parsons School). As a young bride "wishing for something to occupy her days," she studied "piecemeal" between trips to South America with her first husband, Drury McMillen, an engineer. Nevertheless, her talent won her an additional year's scholarship (she accepted the award but asked that the stipend be given to another, needy student). The six months she spent in Paris studying under William Odom made them mutual admirers, and eventually they became business partners as well. From France Odom sent home the antiques and accessories that she first sold out of her town house.

The Odom chairs have become part of the McMillen idiom, as has the lacquered and gilded eighteenth-century Venetian secretary that has been in Mrs. Brown's own apartment for years. In 1989 the secretary, the Odom chairs, and several other pieces were chosen by a major furniture manufacturer, Baker, to be the prototypes for the "McMillen Collection," a group of reproductions intended for collectors of somewhat lesser means than the firm's usual clients. A list of those clients reads like a veritable who's who: Fricks, Fords, Dukes, Vanderbilts, the Marshall Fields, Mrs. Marjorie Merriweather Post, and Millicent Rogers, plus a number of major corporate clients, including the U.S. Government (McMillen redid six rooms in Blair House for the Kennedy administration, and returned to decorate the Johnsons' private quarters in the White House).

But then, the company is used to having clients return for additional work over the years. McMillen has done thirteen successive houses for Anne Ford, for example, and in some cases is now working for the grandchildren of its original clients.

Through it all — through the segues from Art Deco to International Modernism to Contemporary to the English country-house revival of the 1980s — the "McMillen look" may have flexed a bit to accommodate new ideas. But its founder's credo, as recorded in *The World of McMillen,* still holds sway:

The basic rules of proportion and scale are unchanging. . . . They are reinterpreted according to the needs of the time. I like simplicity and I believe in restraint. Above all, there should be harmony — of proportion, line, color, and feeling. The most important element in decorating is the relationship between objects — in size, form, texture, color, and meaning.   □

Before she moved into her apartment, Mrs. Brown reordered the architecture, shaping the dining room into an oval, with four niches, mirrored walls, and a floor of green and white marble. The French Directoire chairs are covered in leather.

Opposite: Even when McMillen, Incorporated, interpreted contemporary trends, the result was classic. Only the chenille covers on the chairs and sofa suggest that this room was done in the 1930s.
(Photographs courtesy McMillen, Incorporated)

Above: Always classic, yet always moving
with the times, McMillen, Incorporated,
romanticized this living room, designed for
Millicent Rogers in the 1930s. The walls were
swagged in crimson silk, with an antique
needlepoint rug on the floor.

Right: A client's bedroom walls were
covered in fabric in the early 1960s to create
a quiet background for an extraordinary
black and gold lacquer Regency tester bed.

Opposite: Smoked mirrors line a hallway in
a house designed for the Alfred Gwynne
Vanderbilts in the 1950s. Mirrors remain one
of the firm's trademarks. The drawings in the
hall are by Van Day Truex.
(Photographs courtesy
McMillen, Incorporated)

To frame a splendid view of the East River in a client's apartment, McMillen lavishes a window with flowers and fringe. The open armchairs are Louis-Philippe, in black lacquer; the rug is a modern copy of a Persian design.

Left: The "McMillen, Incorporated, look," as seen in the drawing room of company president Betty Sherrill, is "American eclectic," she says, drawing on all style sources. One of a pair of eighteenth-century English chairs sits before a Louis XVI desk. The fauteuils are eighteenth-century French; eighteenth-century Chippendale mirrors hang over a pair of painted Adam consoles, also from the eighteenth century.

Mrs. Sherrill's leopard-print dining room was claimed from former maids' rooms. The Odom-designed upholstered armchairs, here ranged around a nineteenth-century French table, are now available in reproduction. The candlesticks and epergne are one of a signed pair by Thornir. The walls are covered with silver-leaf tea paper.

Opposite: The animal-print theme continues in the library, on upholstered furniture and cushions. The painting under the trophy head is by Dunoyer de Segonzac. The chinoiserie chest is English Regency; eighteenth-century Italian chairs surround a game table from nineteenth-century France. The spiral table is another McMillen signature.

"Old, beautiful, romantic, and lush"

ROSE CUMMING

If thwarted romance got Rose Cumming into decorating, as the story goes, it was romance — full-blown and fully realized — that characterized her work.

Caught in New York by World War I, with her fiancé on the other side of the Atlantic, the young Miss Cumming was in the right place at the right time, and she made the most of it on her own, highly individualistic terms. Decorating other people's homes — for pay — was still a new concept. The few women then at work could be considered classicists. Certainly Elsie de Wolfe knew her eighteenth-century French furniture, as well as the teachings of the architect Odgen Codman, Jr. As Elsie's protégé, so did Ruby Ross Wood. Nancy McClelland was Vassar-educated and had studied art history in Paris, and Eleanor McMillen Brown was among the students being trained according to the classical disciplines at the New York School.

Rose Cumming had *flair* instead. And flair proved to be all that was necessary for her to attract both attention and famous clients, among them Marlene Dietrich and Mary Pickford. "Rose always said that all a school could really teach you was what color *not* to put in a north room," her sister and partner, Eileen Cumming Cecil, once related.

There were few don'ts in Rose Cumming's decorating vocabulary. Wall-to-wall carpeting was one of them: instead of what she called " 'ere to 'ere," her rooms had bare and gleaming wood floors. Color — and a colorful mixture of furnishings, from any and all periods — was everywhere else in a Rose Cumming room. In an era marked by quiet hues, she "unbeiged" everything, lavishing windows with yards of billowing taffetas, chintzes, and shimmering silks in color combinations that were startling at the time. She thought nothing of using cosmos pink, lilac, and electric blue in the same room, reasoning that if "parrots are blue and green, why shouldn't fabrics be?" Such colors were unheard-of, so she had her own fabrics dyed and sold them — at exorbitant prices — to other decorators through the shop she opened on Madison Avenue in 1921.

"Everything in the shop was broken, cracked, or falling down," remembers one New York designer, "but it was wonderful to go in and rummage around. You could find the most delightful things tucked away everywhere."

Happily and totally eclectic in her collecting, Rose once wrote, "I love everything that is beautiful, no matter whether it is fish or fowl. My loves," she said in an understatement, "are passionate and legion." She found her "loves" everywhere she went and brought them back to the cluttered treasury that was her shop for more than forty-five years. Ronald Grimaldi, the president of Rose Cumming, Incorporated, recalls the time she came home from a trip to New England with a crystal chandelier tied to the roof of her chauffeur-driven limousine.

Her approach to arranging rooms was equally unorthodox. "Decorating is a trial-and-error thing," she wrote, "like trying on hats until you find the one that fits." Rose's method was a matter of "pulling and dragging everything back and forth, trying objects here and there, until I find the exact place in the room where this or that piece looks best — and there it stays forever."

A large, strong woman, Rose often did much of the hefting herself. She also lifted the horizons of interior decorating. Venturing well beyond the bounds of correct period rooms, she added a dimension of individualism and lyrical romanticism that lingers on in Manhattan Style today. □

Rose Cumming once wrote, "With passion I love pure colors: fresh, brilliant, and clear colors." It was a passion she indulged full-tilt when she created this sitting room for herself in the 1930s, with emerald walls and cobalt upholstery. The furnishings were equally colorful: the painted chairs are eighteenth-century Portuguese; the japanned secretary is English, of the Queen Anne period. (Photograph courtesy Rose Cumming, Incorporated)

Right: A woman who actually enjoyed polishing her own floors, Rose Cumming was fond of sparkle and shine. Here she mirrored nearly every surface in a dressing room that opens into an entry hall. The pair of lacquer altar tables are Chinese.

Opposite: Mirrored panels in her foyer on West Fifty-fourth Street multiply the effect of the Chinese temple pagoda and marble goddesses, over which hangs an eighteenth-century crystal chandelier in the form of a galleon.

Below: If Rose Cumming did not invent eclecticism, she certainly advanced its cause in her own gleaming silver and blue bedroom. The windows and the sixteenth-century Portuguese bed are hung with lamé; the low table was a child's bed in eighteenth-century Persia, and the silver-plated Moorish stools and tables are thought to have belonged to Catherine the Great. (Photographs courtesy Rose Cumming, Incorporated)

All of Rose Cumming's rooms had star quality, but none more so than this dressing room. Designed in 1934, it featured black wallpaper sprinkled with stars.

Opposite: Bare floors and the bold use of color in lavish fabrics were among the designer's other signatures. In her mother's bedroom, done in the 1930s, she combined two shades of lilac taffeta on the *lit à la polonaise,* introduced blue and pink, and summed up all the colors in the chintz curtains and headboard. (Photographs courtesy Rose Cumming, Incorporated)

"If it looks right, it is right!"

DOROTHY DRAPER

Standing well over six feet tall, with fox furs thrown around her shoulders and feathers nodding on her hat, Dorothy Draper pressed her credo upon the homemakers of America for some forty years, and they listened gratefully. A grande dame by any measure, New York–born and with unquestionable social credentials, connections, and old money behind her, Mrs. Draper brought the very concept of interior decorating to the masses through her books, radio programs, and national newspaper and magazine columns. Just as surely, she brought the masses in to witness her own decorating achievements as one of the first designers to focus on public spaces and consumer products.

The hotels Mrs. Draper designed were not only commercial successes that quickly drew admiring crowds, they also helped change the attitude of the hotel industry. Stiff, businesslike bedrooms became comfortable sitting rooms; lobbies and ballrooms became *theater*, larger-than-life settings that radiated glamour and generated excitement. Mrs. Draper operated on a grand scale, on *over-scale* — employing vast cabbbage-rose chintzes, giant lamps, and great white-plaster ornamental appliqués, most often against her favored dark-green or dark-burgundy walls. "Neobaroque" it might have been called, the intrepid creation of an imperious, untrained society lady, the wife of a doctor and mother of three who disdained antiques in favor of "jumbling periods cheerfully" and who thought nothing of telling a client to dye a good Oriental rug or to paint fine old mahogany furniture rhododendron pink.

But the American public loved both her and her style. During the 1940s Dorothy Draper became literally a household word, as director of *Good Housekeeping*'s Studio for Living and the author of a regular column for the magazine, in which she offered advice and assurances on everything from interior decorating to positive thinking.

One of the first interior decorators to lend her talents to the business world, she designed products as diverse as fabrics and wallpaper (for Schumacher), rugs (for Heritage), furniture (for Henredon), and airplane interiors (for Convair). Often she lent her name — and her social prestige — as well, appearing in advertisements for the 1952 Packard for which she had styled the interior and imprinting her signature rose on a wildly popular line of cosmetics for Dorothy Gray.

It is a mark of her success — as her successor, Carleton Varney, points out — that over one hundred years after her birth, in 1889, and more than twenty years after her death, in 1969, examples of Mrs. Draper's work are still plentiful. The Hampshire House on Central Park South retains both her baroque appliqués and her dramatically scaled flooring designs, as do a number of the apartment-house lobbies she designed along Park Avenue. At the Metropolitan Museum of Art, only the massive birdcage chandeliers remain in the cafeteria that was nicknamed the "Dorotheum" after she did it up in grandiose style, marching columns around a Roman pool upon which sculptured figures danced. But the lobbies of the Carlyle Hotel, where Mrs. Draper also lived, retain her floor scheme and her late Art Deco detailing, even though the colors and furnishings have since been changed.

"Dorothy Draper had both exquisite taste and a certain kind of guts," says Varney, who wrote a book about his mentor that was published the year before the centennial of her birth.

"At a time when people were afraid to do anything colorful or interesting, she was big, colorful, and bold!" □

Typical Dorothy Draperisms in her own Carlyle Hotel apartment in the early 1950s: exuberant cabbage roses within dark plum walls, with a white baroque fireplace of her design. The portrait is of her great-great-grandmother Anna Mary Wendell (Mrs. Robert Bowne Minturn). (Photograph courtesy Carleton Varney)

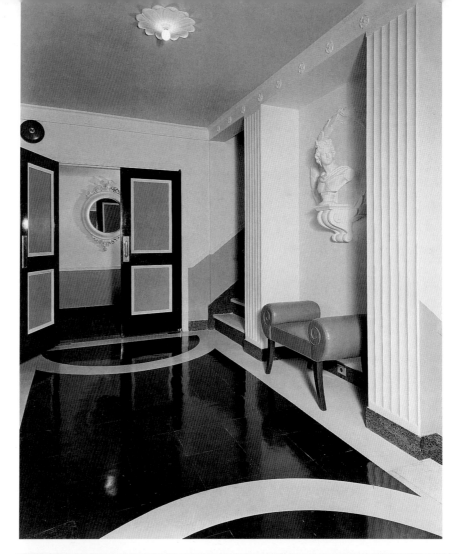

Above: Under a sky-blue ceiling, Dorothy Draper created an elevator lobby of invigorating contrasts, featuring black and white rubber-tile floors, dead-white walls, and gray dados and doors. The bench is a shock of red leather with jumbo welting.

Right: Neobaroque plaster decorations set on a mirror surround the glass moulding of a fireplace in the Hampshire House lobby. Even the fringe on the wing chairs carried Mrs. Draper's exaggerated scale to almost surrealistic dimensions.

Opposite: Living with her own trademarks, Mrs. Draper strewed cabbage roses over her bedroom in the Carlyle Hotel and covered the floor with white carpeting. The two phones were necessities for a career woman of the day. (Photographs courtesy Carleton Varney)

"Discipline — always my motto"

MRS. HENRY PARISH II

She may be known as "Sister," but to generations of interior designers Mrs. Henry Parish II is also a "godmother" and the "grandmother of us all."

Others call her "an institution," "a legend," "a genius," and "the grande dame" of design.

Dorothy Kinnicutt Parish accepts it all with an indulgent smile. Behind such accolades — also lavished upon her by some of America's richest and most famous, her clients — is something else Sister understands well: hard work.

The fact that she was to the manor born — and that the manor belonged to an old, wealthy, and influential family — accounts for only the beginning of her success. The talent was inborn, and the feeling for elegant, comfortable rooms and a gracious way of life ingrained. Certainly Sister would have gone on living that life in New Jersey, New York, and Dark Harbor, Maine, if the stock market crash of 1929 had not ruined her husband and father. Never mind that wellborn women of the day did not work, and that decorating was a fledgling profession, if that; Sister rolled up her silk sleeves and helped write its history.

But again, that was only the beginning. Some sixty years later, her style remains classic, but not static. She has not only moved with the times, she has led the way, continuing to create rooms that are as fresh and romantic as they are elegant and comfortable, working for some of the wealthiest and most demanding clients in the country. Such names as Astor, Kennedy, Getty, Kissinger, and Haupt crowd the firm's client roster. York — as in the Duke and Duchess of — nearly joined them. The royal couple were charmed by the Parish approach to the "English manor house" look and wanted to hire the American company to do their new home.

It didn't happen — an English decorator got the job, of course — but the story confirms what Mrs. Parish's clients have known for years: she is able to translate perfectly not only the decoration of grand rooms in the easy-living English manner, but the very *essence* of manor life as well.

And it's all done by instinct, something Mrs. Parish believes in firmly. "I don't think a decorator can learn taste," she says. "You either have it, or you don't." Of herself she has insisted, "I'm only a pro in my eye; I never could hold a pencil." That is left to Albert Hadley, a former Parsons professor and her partner since 1962. His approach has been called intellectual, contrapuntal to her innate "flair." Together they have kept Parish-Hadley Associates in the forefront of the design profession worldwide.

Certainly the firm has been a major training ground for other top decorators now working on their own, including Mark Hampton, Kevin McNamara, David Easton, and Mariette Himes Gomez. Parish-Hadley has even been called a "finishing school" in the old tradition carried on at Parsons earlier in the century.

So, too, have many of Sister Parish's ideas found their way into the mainstream of interior design. She is credited with popularizing the use of American quilts as decorative art (and, in the process, creating an important cottage industry in the South). Even putting flowers in ordinary baskets was a surprise when she first did it.

Over the years, such small gestures have enlarged the decorator's reputation for genius. If these touches look effortless, that has always been the charm of a Sister Parish room. It is a look achieved through a lifetime of determination, caring, and plain old hard work. "Discipline," she has said, "has always been my motto.

"If my 'Undecorated Look' has meant rooms that are personal, comfortable, friendly, and gay, I feel I have accomplished a great deal." □

When she lived on East Seventy-ninth Street during the 1960s, Mrs. Parish lined the dining-room walls with trompe l'oeil painted canvas that had been removed from a Kinnicutt family apartment in Paris. (Photograph courtesy Parish-Hadley Associates)

Opposite: The drawing room on East Seventy-ninth Street featured a pair of English pine corner cupboards against walls enameled dark brown. The late-eighteenth-century mirror, a family heirloom, is one of a pair still in Mrs. Parish's possession. (Photograph courtesy Parish-Hadley Associates)

Below: In the library of the Fifth Avenue maisonette where she now lives — and which once belonged to Gloria Swanson — Mrs. Parish evokes her trademark country-in-the-city elegance. The center of attention is the eighteenth-century English secretary with its doors open against the bookshelves.

A portrait of Mrs. Parish looks over the drawing room of her maisonette, which is arranged to provide many intimate seating areas, a hallmark of her style over the years. An heirloom eighteenth-century English mirror, one of a pair, hangs by the window. Flanking the fireplace are a pair of late-eighteenth-century girandoles. The carpet is an Aubusson; hand-painted silk and velvet pillows, another Parish signature, are gathered on the damask-covered sofa and chair.

Dining in the style that he helped to originate: Truex set a modern version of the Parsons table and pulled up chairs designed by Jean-Michel Frank, covered in leopard-print fabric.

Below: A designer who had an extraordinary way with the ordinary, Van Day Truex used yards and yards of humble mattress ticking throughout his own apartment in 1953. His version of "peasant chic" quickly launched a trend among Parsons students of the day.

"Control. Distill. Edit."

VAN DAY TRUEX

His name still comes up often in discussions of taste and style. Van Day Truex, who headed the Parsons program in Paris during the 1930s and was president of the school itself from 1942 to 1953, exerted an enormous — and lasting — influence on design directions in New York for more than half a century.

His influence came not only from his teachings but from the life he lived and the manner in which he insisted upon living it, as well as from the practical application of his firmly held tenets when he left the field of education to become design director of Tiffany & Company for a dozen decisive years. During his tenure there the most everyday objects became *objets d'art*: doorknobs, bottles, and forks and knives and spoons were rethought, at his urging, by such major artists as Noguchi and Léger — and by Truex himself — and redesigned into things of beauty to enhance life and the living thereof.

The quest for quality, in things and in life-style, was the legacy Truex left the generations of designers who came under his aegis. It was, perhaps, an ideal that Truex had adopted from William Odom, his own mentor and predecessor at Parsons. But Truex, who came from Kansas and maintained an engaging down-home accent and attitude all his life, brought another, warm dimension to the grandeur that so impressed his students. A midwestern practicality tempered the otherworldliness of the glittering social life he lived in New York and abroad. He believed that taste could be taught and developed continually; he tended to laugh at his own fanaticisms — particularly for order and scale — and was convinced that the quality of design in the marketplace was entirely the responsibility of designers and manufacturers. "Provide less, provide better," he wrote.

Once known as an "avant garde traditionalist," Truex brought European ideas to America, and vice versa. He knew the no-color work of the designer Syrie Maugham and loved, wore, and lived with beige all his life.

An American in Paris — and a poor American at that — Truex turned his predilection for blue jeans, sneakers, and seersucker jacket into "poor chic," an idea that he reexpressed years later in his work for Tiffany. Humble berry baskets were translated into silver and an ordinary Bordeaux bottle was rendered in Baccarat crystal. And when he decorated his own New York apartment in yards and yards of humble mattress ticking — in a poor man's version of Elsie de Wolfe's famous striped room at Villa Trianon — it launched a trend. Parsons students, and the public, watched and learned every time Truex redid his apartment (which was at regular two-year intervals during the 1940s), changing its color schemes dramatically but always applying the credo he drilled into Parsons students: "Control. Edit. Distill."

"I believe in fashion, but it is a power that can get out of hand," Truex said in an interview shortly before his death, in 1979. "One needs to remain aloof, to recognize changes and influences, but to keep at the same time a certain objectivity. This is a view we insisted on at Parsons." □

When he entertained in his small New York pied-à-terre, Truex liked to move the dining "room" to different locations. Here it is shown set up by a window with the "Van *ordinaire*" decanter and all-purpose wineglasses he designed for Tiffany. (Photographs courtesy *House & Garden*)

"The elegance of simplicity and honesty"

BILLY BALDWIN

When Baldwin moved into the newly renovated Amster Yard after the war, he used dark green —"the color of a wet gardenia leaf"— throughout the sitting room. It was, he said, a tribute to Elsie de Wolfe, but the design world soon associated dark green with B.B. himself. "Those walls had a huge influence," recalls Stanley Barrows. "After a photo of Billy's room was published [in 1947], everybody started doing it." (Photograph courtesy *House & Garden*)

When he moved to New York in 1935 to join Ruby Ross Wood's firm, Billy Baldwin became one of the first men to follow the professional trail that had been blazed by a generation of women decorators. By the time he left the city in 1972 to retire on Nantucket, Baldwin had become what the *New York Times* would call "the dean of American interior decorators . . . the greatest influence on a generation of post–World War II designers."

Renowned for his personal elegance — an admirer once described him as a "small but exquisite jewel" — Baldwin grew up among the "right" families in Baltimore and tried, for two unsatisfying years, to study architecture at Princeton. But, he later recalled, he "was always spending time in New York at museums and galleries and things." A stint at his father's insurance company finally convinced him to pursue his first love, and he had already developed a solid decorating practice in Baltimore by the time Mrs. Wood called to offer him thirty-five dollars a week and the use of her New York apartment while he settled into the business.

"When she asked me to work for her, Mrs. Wood said she had never thought of hiring a man," Baldwin wrote. "In those days, all the leading decorators were women . . . [and] Heaven knows, these women had absolutely marvelous taste, but most of it was based on the eighteenth century and eighteenth-century antiques."

"Billy B.," as he was known to friends, was overjoyed to get out of Maryland and eighteenth-century England and into the "modern Continental world" that was Manhattan in the 1930s. "New York was a wonderland for me," he said. "I was in revolt against Baltimore, a town in which there could not have been more than three or four French chairs. I didn't want to be stuck doing Chippendale all my life — I wanted to do high style."

He was to revise his definition of "high style" significantly over the course of the next forty years, but he was always quick to credit his mentor, Mrs. Wood, for providing him with the basis of his decorating philosophy: "Ruby had three credos, and all three of them were unbelievably simple. First, she never let you lose sight of the

personal in decorating. Second, comfort. Third and last, the new. She made you aware of the importance of the new design or the new color or the new whatever . . . but she also made you select only what you considered best and always cast aside the novelty."

In his own work, Baldwin cast aside clichés and redefined the meaning of luxury, which he believed many people confused with grandeur. The latter was never part of his decorating vocabulary, despite the fact that his clients included many of the mid–twentieth century's wealthiest and most world-famous figures: he decorated for Cole Porter, Diana Vreeland, the Paul Mellons, S. I. Newhouse, Jr., and Jacqueline Onassis, to cite only a few. But he refused to spend their money unnecessarily, preferring, as *Vogue*'s editor Diana Vreeland said, "to do much with not too much, to let a little go a long way. He didn't arbitrarily throw out your furniture and used as much of it as possible if it was any good in the first place."

He also advocated having furniture upholstered right to the floor, saying that "a roomful of chair legs looks so restless." He warned against what he called the "sterility of perfection," adding that "nothing is interesting unless it is personal." Finally, while he admired English and French decorators — Jean-Michel Frank in particular — Baldwin was a great believer in the American look. As he wrote in an article for *House & Garden* toward the end of his career,

American decorating has been uniquely itself. We have tended to simplify, to give rooms a fresher, younger look. Perhaps because we are a younger country, founded and built by people with open minds and a willingness to take risks. . . . The greatest decorating in America has never been frivolous — it has been built upon solid foundations. Authority is not just a good shot, it's confidence. . . .

As for me, the country boy from Baltimore who wanted to do high style, I find myself interested only in simplicity in every way. . . . We're talking about someplace people live in, surrounded by things they like and that make them comfortable. It's as simple as that. □

The "children of Cole Porter's bookcases," as Billy Baldwin called them, stood at angles to a Korean lacquer screen in the designer's own one-room apartment of 1963. The writing table in the foreground was covered in brown felt that reached to the bare parquet floor.

Right: The "Coromandel brown" color scheme with which Baldwin had a lifelong love affair warmed all the walls in the apartment. The painting of English dogs dates from the early eighteenth century.

Opposite: Although the room measured only twelve by eighteen feet, the designer used a variety of textures to enliven the color scheme. The gleaming brown Louis XV leather chair and gold-touched screen were among Baldwin's favorite possessions. (Photographs courtesy House & Garden)

Billy Baldwin called the brass bookshelves he created for Cole Porter's study, in the Waldorf Towers, his "most enduring design." The shelves fronted the tortoiseshell-painted walls on three sides and served as a backdrop for the French antiques the Porters had collected when they lived in Paris during the 1920s.

Right: The bookshelves — and his signature brown walls — stayed when Baldwin "uncluttered" his own Sixty-second Street apartment in 1973. The white rug and cream-colored glazed-chintz shades were added "to calm things down," he said. (Photographs courtesy *House & Garden*)

Diana Vreeland told Billy Baldwin that she wanted him to
turn her apartment into a "garden in hell." He obliged
by covering nearly everything in a scarlet chintz with brilliant ·
Persian flowers, found in John Fowler's shop in London.
(Photograph courtesy Lizzie Himmel)

Paneled walls and gilt mirrors gave a European lilt to the future baroness's bedroom when she lived in New York in 1943. The silver screen was Japanese.

Below: Although the apartment had only two rooms, Pauline Potter's singular sense of style caught the attention of the design media. Her living room was centered around a large eighteenth-century Persian rug and a Louis XV desk. On the chimneypiece are Chinese export porcelains. (Photographs courtesy *Vogue*)

"Le Style Pauline"

PAULINE de ROTHSCHILD

Billy Baldwin was an admiring friend, always insisting that she had given him early lessons in decorating. Sister Parish cites her "feeling for quality and sense of style." And the design media of the world gave up trying to describe her talent and took to calling it simply "Le Style Pauline."

Pauline Potter — later married to the aesthetic vintner Baron Philippe de Rothschild, of the French banking family — never decorated professionally. Her design career per se was spent in the world of fashion, with Schiaparelli and Hattie Carnegie, but her celebrated individuality influenced even influential decorators during her years in New York.

"She had her own way of looking at things, and it was very personal," the designer Mel Dwork remembers, "strictly to please herself, her husband, and friends." For instance, she hung magnificent Chinese panels on the *inside* of her closet doors. "They were there to give *her* joy when she opened them," Dwork says. "Pauline never did anything just to impress."

After all, whom did she need to impress? An American whose childhood was spent in Paris, she returned — as an orphan — to make her debut in Baltimore, courtesy of relatives there.

Quite tall and model-slender, Pauline established herself as a natural tastemaker from that moment on. When she and her first husband lived in Majorca before the Spanish civil war, she opened a chic little shop that sold fashions and handcrafts made by the natives. Driven back to New York by the war — and divorced — she soon made a reputation for herself with her "flair for mixing the previously unmixable," to quote Billy Baldwin.

Originality was to remain her signature when she married the most eligible bachelor in Europe at the time, the poetry-writing, Grand Prix–racing, equally individualistic Baron Philippe de Rothschild, owner of the famed Château Mouton vineyards. Important figures on the political, literary, and theatrical scenes of three continents could be found around the Rothschilds' tables in Bordeaux and Paris, from their marriage, in 1954, until Pauline's death, in 1976. The tables themselves even made news: for centerpieces, the Baroness designed small, exquisite landscapes.

Not only these "woodland fantasies" but the very way she made *living* itself a fine art were highly original, sometimes even startling. As Billy Baldwin maintained, she was the "personification of American spontaneity, freshness, and style." □

Always an acclaimed hostess, Mrs. Potter dined on a collapsible table in a corner of the living room, beneath her cherished Vuillard paintings. At this point she insisted on keeping the table free of the fresh flowers that would become her trademark at Château Mouton. (Photograph courtesy Vogue)

"A knowing eye"

STANLEY BARROWS

He has been called the éminence grise of American interior design, the man who taught — or was taught by — the true lights in the field. At home on the East Side, "The Professor" lives surrounded by thousands of books and the souvenirs of a life of travel and discerning, classic taste.

Not least among those souvenirs are vivid memories of many of the earlier decorators who brought the profession into the mainstream of Manhattan life. There was Rose Cumming, a "femme forte — she loved physical work, loved getting up at five to wax the floors. Rose expanded decorating beyond the boundaries of interior design. I used to send my students to take notes on her window displays, juxtapositions of things suggesting a wonderful room. They could change a student's mind overnight!"

Barrows was there when Billy Baldwin shared floor plans, problems, and solutions with Parsons students, often opening the doors to his own apartment so they could see his work.

And Barrows recalls how the legendary Jean-Michel Frank, in Paris, reduced the table to its pure components — legs, top, legs — and created what became known as the Parsons table.

"Frank was a critic at the Paris program — critics came several times a year and lectured," Barrows recalls. "The gratin of Paris would come to study. Frank showed how simple a table could be — just this, this, and this." He draws the silhouette in the air. "But he also showed how that simple shape could be finished in wonderful, different ways. Parisian decorators would send their cabinetmakers to copy those 'Parsons' tables."

A legend talking about legends, Barrows has also taught a number of the important designers who followed, among them Albert Hadley, Tom Britt, Angelo Donghia . . . and many others who name "The Professor" as inspiration for their careers. Most of them carry forth the classic tradition of the Parsons School, where Barrows himself first studied and then taught for twenty-two years.

"I was the last student to darken the door of 9 Place des Vosges," he says. Built in 1625, the elegant Paris branch of the school was presided over at that time by the even more elegant William

Odom, a traditionalist's traditionalist who took his students to see, study, and meticulously measure many of the great houses in France and Italy. For the most part privately owned, opened to Odom through his far-reaching social connections, these great houses exerted a great influence on an entire generation of American designers. Barrows's own studies, however, were cut short.

"It was the summer of '39, and we were in Italy when Odom got a telegram: 'Come back. The war is starting in two days.' And it did! I'd left my trunks, skis, and gramophone in Paris, and to get them I had to take a midnight train from Switzerland. Its windows were painted blue and there were machine gunners front and back. It was the first time I took the war seriously."

He could not get serious about his own design career until after the war. And then it was as a teacher, rather than a practitioner, that he left his imprint on the field. Returning from the armed forces, the young designer went to see Van Day Truex, another important influence on him, who had become president of Parsons when Odom died, in 1942. "Van invited me to come teach. I thought I'd stay to the end of the semester."

Instead, he stayed until 1968, directing the European Studies program and passing on a feeling for the discipline, order, and balance of classic eighteenth-century design. Other Barrows protégés came from the Fashion Institute of Technology in New York. When Parsons, as Barrows says, "moved away from residential design toward space-planning and problem-solving," he became head of FIT's interior design department, a position he held for seventeen years.

Now he allows himself a small smile of satisfaction at the fact that contemporary design is swinging back toward the teaching of the classics. Barrows, of course, is not surprised. "Simplicity, order, and flexibility endure through the centuries. The eighteenth century was disciplined, it was rational, and, I have always thought, it had an important design message to give the twentieth century. . . .

"No," Barrows amends, definitely a man who keeps up with the times. "Make that the twenty-first century." □

Part of Barrows's collection of books, some five thousand strong, overflows the English Regency boulle bookcase made by Jean Berain from Louis XIV designs. The garniture on top is blue-and-white Chinese. The early-nineteenth-century engravings are by Rossi; the table in the foreground is American, a family heirloom.

The Chinese red lacquer drop-front desk sits beneath a small portrait of Sir James Thornhill, painted by Hogarth's daughter. The porcelains are Chinese and Dutch delft.

Below: In the dining area, Italian Empire chairs from the early nineteenth century surround a glass and chrome table set with Wedgwood dessert plates. A pair of lacquer Chinese export chairs flank the marquetry commode, made in southern France in the mid–eighteenth century; on top is a collection of hard stone, malachite, and rock-crystal figurines.

Underneath his collection of disparate and very personal objects, Barrows's apartment is organized according to the classic laws of proportion and symmetry. Carefully balanced on a Portuguese needlepoint rug from the late seventeenth century are a 1935 chesterfield sofa with two beaded Victorian Berlin-work pillows, two Italian lamps, and two gilt bronze tables, which came from Syrie Maugham.

"Working from the bones up"

ALBERT HADLEY

It is a question he has been asked many times in the long course of an illustrious career at the very top of the interior design profession. But Albert Hadley taps another unfiltered cigarette from the pack on his desk at Parish-Hadley Associates, and then considers his answer through a swirl of smoke.

"Does my work have a particularly identifiable 'look'? Yes, I suppose it does," he responds finally. "I'm told that it can be identified by a certain clarity, a cleanness that comes from having a purposeful point of view."

A former teacher at Parsons — where he also studied — and still quietly donnish, Hadley has passed on that purposeful point of view to other members of the firm. That is one reason he prefers to talk about Parish-Hadley Associates' work rather than his own. The word *I* seldom comes up when he is discussing design; the proper pronoun is *we*, as in "What *we* strive for is a sense of order, of quality, rather than some particular hallmark."

That sense of order begins with the architecture of whatever room is on the drawing board at the time. It is a process that Hadley has called "working from the bones up." Without the proper respect for architecture, Hadley believes, a designer is merely decorating the surface, "just filling the place with pretty things and letting it go at that."

"Things" per se are not in Hadley's design vocabulary. Ask him about the ongoing vogue for the cozy clutter of the "English country house" look, and he smiles, maintaining, "There *is* an overabundance of exuberance in some of today's decorating." Yet his own apartment is a rich collection of objects, some important, many simply amusing and whimsical, as is the designer himself.

"Nothing in there is worth a thing — except to me," Hadley demurs. "The apartment is a private place. I guess you could call it a scrapbook of

friendships," he says, eyes smiling behind owlish round glasses.

Scrapbooks figure in both Hadley's private and professional lives. In his office, a large bulletin board is a riot of colorful scraps, including clippings, swatches, postcards, whatever has caught his eye or fancy. Another, at home, stretching to perhaps eight by six feet, is framed in gilt. At the center of the pastiche is a card that reads: "It is not simply a matter of reaching the top, but going a little higher."

Hadley reached the top early in his career — at least, the top in the design world of his native Nashville, Tennessee. In his first design job he worked as an apprentice to the "fine, old-fashioned decorator A. Herbert Rogers, where I even learned how to upholster." When he came to New York — "going a little higher" — Hadley ran right into Eleanor McMillen Brown's celebrated policy of not hiring anyone who had not been to Parsons. So he enrolled, won the Elsie de Wolfe scholarship to study in Paris, and later returned to teach at the school before finally joining McMillen, Incorporated, in 1956. After five highly successful years there — his clients during that time included Josh Logan and the White House — Hadley took both his talent and his name to Mrs. Parish's firm. Since then he has created a number of rooms that are almost as well known as their owners — the red library for Mrs. Vincent Astor, for example, and the historic living room that he recast for Mrs. Nelson Rockefeller, originally designed by Jean-Michel Frank and the architect Wallace Harrison.

To each of these Hadley brought his "look" — that sense of clarity and discipline and, above all, perhaps, comfort. But each time, he emphasizes, it results in a different room, one distinctly suited to the client. It must.

"You can't decorate by formula," Hadley says. "It's all a question of the discerning eye." □

Albert Hadley's own bedroom has been edited down to the essentials, as seen through the designer's almost Spartan eye: one of his Louis XVI chairs, an L. L. Bean blanket and an assortment of shapes that amuse him, including the nail-studded globe by Armin Postler, a collection of carpentry tools, and a trio of cast-iron garden rabbits from the nineteenth century.

An eighteenth-century Chinese lacquer screen serves as backdrop for the ever-changing display of objects that Hadley enjoys looking at from his bed, including the sculptured metal hand from Karl Springer.

Opposite: In his drawing room, Hadley recessed and mirrored the baseboard and cornice so the silver tea-paper-covered walls appear to float over the dark-stained floor. The pair of Louis XVI bergères are upholstered in pewter satin; the leather-covered Louis XVI chair in front of the window is one of a pair that once belonged to William Odom. The rug is American Indian.

A mirrored sphere, rush matting, and a carved French table
presented an interesting interplay of textures in a corner of
Hadley's earlier apartment.
(Photograph courtesy Parish-Hadley Associates)

Opposite: The study in Hadley's present apartment is also
a study in contrasts: the eighteenth-century Louis XVI chair
is upholstered in an American Indian blanket from the
nineteenth century; the tiered bookcase is German, from
the early twentieth century. Helene Fessenmeier
made the prints.

In his own apartment of thirty years ago, Hadley combined *faux bois* print fabric on the chairs with an animal-print rug and an American quilt. The torchères and sconces once belonged to Syrie Maugham; the sconces are still in Hadley's office at Parish-Hadley.

Right: Walls of mirror mosaics in the bath reflected Hadley's unorthodox way of combining materials and textures. (Photographs courtesy Parish-Hadley Associates)

The dolphin-based table, set against
silver tea-paper walls in the same apartment,
also came from Syrie Maugham. The chairs
flanking the table are English Regency.
(Photograph courtesy Parish-Hadley
Associates)

Homage to understatement

GARY HAGER
FOR
PARISH-HADLEY

It's a long way from the antiques-filled Victorian country house Gary Hager grew up in to the "symmetry, simplicity, and restraint" that he now practices for the New York design firm Parish-Hadley Associates. In a sense, Hager made the transition by limousine — he started his career with the firm as a chauffeur — bringing along his appreciation for the past, learned in his parents' home. The elder Hagers were antiques dealers in East Aurora, New York, the small town that was the center of the American Arts and Crafts movement around the turn of the century.

"That was a fun house to grow up in," Hager recalls. "We rearranged the rooms every few months — everyone even changed bedrooms."

In his work for Parish-Hadley, the designer has developed a new perspective on the past. He still works with antiques from myriad sources and centuries, but now he uses them in a decidedly modern manner.

"You can't help but draw from the past," he says, "but *ornate* is not necessarily elegant and refined." What *is*, by the designer's definition: space — orderly, tightly edited space that lends a classic calm to the rooms he designs.

"Space is such a luxury, why give it up to clutter and confusion?" he asks. It is no surprise that Hager's commitment to the "thorough and systematic replacement of unworthy detail" stems from his admiration for the work of Jean-Michel Frank, the French master of understatement. In fact, the Gracie Square apartment that Hager designed for clients who shared that admiration is a palimpsest of the celebrated townhouse Frank created for the Vicomte and Vicomtesse de Noailles in Paris in 1932.

Hager calls his clients "brave," and the resulting apartment "one of the best things I've done. I knew the clients, I knew the space, and I knew what I wanted to do here. Frank is so modern. I'd taken inspiration from his work before, but never so completely."

The designer reordered the architecture of the thirties apartment, raising and widening doorways (the doorknobs are set low to enhance the illusion of height) and editing out extraneous detail. The French-style chimneypiece went; in its stead is a simple stroke of carved limestone with a standing glass screen. Meticulous detailing — a direct homage to Frank — shows up in the nearly bare entrance hall: Hager says it took twenty-six different colors of paint, applied in squares and then glazed, to emulate Frank's trademark parchment wall coverings. The dining-room wall is silver-leafed in squares. Uncarpeted and sparsely furnished, the room projects the same "timeless monumentality" that Frank was renowned for.

For other clients with other demands, Hager's approach may be less severe, but it is no less disciplined. After all, after his short-lived career as a driver at Parish-Hadley, and before he began taking on projects of his own for the firm, Hager spent eight years working closely with Albert Hadley, a modern master of restraint.

In designing, Hager says he simply reaches for "whatever elements seem most pleasing. Often," he points out, "that means selecting modern objects and injecting them into an environment steeped in history."

History, yes, but in Hager's book it will be history reedited and formally balanced. □

An entry hall in homage to Jean-Michel Frank: it took more than twenty different colors of paint and glazes to approximate the richness of Frank's wall coverings, according to Gary Hager. The carved and gilt wood torchère is derivative of a design by Giacometti. The drawing and chair are both by Josef Hoffmann.

In the spare dining room, the walls are covered in squares of silver tea paper, a Parish-Hadley signature that also has overtones of Jean-Michel Frank's work. Hager designed the mirror and the marble table with seams of gilded wood.

Opposite: Art mirrors life in the sitting room overlooking the East River and its bridges. The painting is by Yvonne Jacquette; the leather backgammon table is by Parish-Hadley.

Opposite: Hager intermingles contemporary art
and eighteenth-century antiques against an
all-cream background in a large Sutton Place
apartment. The wing chairs flanking the
fireplace are signed pieces by Jacob. The
English gilt mirrors hang over a pair of
consoles from Italy. The painting on the far
wall is by Lichtenstein, and the one at left, by
Warhol.

Above: Looking the other way, into the
music room: the string carpet and the painted
wall paneling meld the two spaces into one.
Here, both paintings are by Warhol; the
eighteenth-century gilt bronze elephant clock
on the mantel is French; the chair is Swedish,
also from the eighteenth century.

"First of all, I design for people"

ANGELO DONGHIA

In the early 1970s, Donghia designed a dramatic floor of inlaid vinyl for his town house and covered the ceiling in silver leaf. The genial groupings he arranged about the room included his very first designs for furniture. (Photograph courtesy Donghia Associates)

In the 1950s, the young Angelo Donghia looked at the world of design in New York and saw a world of opportunity that extended well beyond the upscale homes of private clients. Over the next quarter century he went on to nationwide fame as the first interior designer to translate the custom-made look into home furnishings for the mass market, establishing an interlocking series of companies to provide goods and services relating to all aspects of the design industry.

By the time he died, in 1985, he had become a "one-man conglomerate," as one columnist put it. But despite the unprecedented scope of the company that Donghia created, his successors still retain the founder's obsession with fine detail.

Donghia was, before anything else, the son of a tailor. He knew the great difference between *acceptable* and *superior* quality, and he built an empire by insisting on the latter. "I like to have control," he once told an interviewer. "I like to be aware of every detail of every project my firm works on." Both the furnishings he designed and the rooms into which he put them were so serenely uncluttered that details became enormously important. Trained at Parsons, steeped in classicism, and highly disciplined, Donghia stressed simplicity of line, purity of materials, and boldness of form, in rooms that appeared "at first sleek and modern, but were actually based on the eighteenth-century belief in sensible proportions and careful symme-

try," in the words of Stanley Barrows, Donghia's teacher at Parsons.

These "sensible proportions" translated into comfort, something Donghia also insisted upon. "I design for people," he maintained. "Rooms are backgrounds for people: that's why they're called living rooms."

Renowned for his sartorial style (he was elected to the International Best Dressed List Hall of Fame in 1977), Donghia made menswear fabrics a personal signature. The plump, rounded chairs that he covered with gray flannel took on what one critic called a "curious" sensuality. When Donghia designed windowpane-checked sheets for a major manufacturer, they became a ten-year sensation. And when he began paring his rooms down to bare, gleaming floors and barely dressed windows, a new standard was set.

In fact, Donghia was reviving an old aesthetic, traceable to his avowed inspiration, Jean-Michel Frank. He also emulated Frank's use of vellum applied to the wall in squares, still a hallmark of Donghia's design firm, as is the concern with creating what Donghia referred to as "total environments."

"Designers work with chairs and tables, of course," he told an interviewer a year before his death. "But we also work with human beings, their bodies, their feelings, their desires to be comfortable and happy, and to survive . . . in comfort and dignity. That's how I see it." □

Donghia's famous green room underwent a number of color changes — from green to white to mauve — before he turned it to green again. "Rooms tell you what to do," he commented, "and that room wanted to be green." It was one of the few times he ever used such extroverted color in his work.

Opposite: Donghia's boldly striped fabric caught the design world's attention when he introduced it in the 1970s. In his own town house, it was visually the equal of the floor's supercharged black-and-white checks. As his career unfolded, Donghia was to lean more toward subtler contrasts and textures.
(Photographs courtesy Donghia Associates)

DANIEL PARKE
FOR
DONGHIA ASSOCIATES

Donghia Associates designer Daniel Parke recast an East Side apartment in warm colors and rich textures that are reminiscent of the 1930s. Working in Donghia's own idiom, he draped slipper chairs in leather, mirrored the fireplace wall, and used black sailcloth bordering white sisal matting for a rug. The andirons are by Giacometti; the Roman vessel on the pedestal dates from the third century B.C.

At first the duplex apartment seems to embody the antithesis of the sensual modernity for which designer Angelo Donghia is remembered. Eighteenth-century antiques and an "English country house" atmosphere dominate the gracious enfilade of rooms seen through arched doorways. Complementary arched windows, dressed in traditional festoons, look out over the city equivalent of a country garden, tree-lined terraces that wrap all around the East Side apartment.

A careful analysis, however, reveals another dimension that gives the English traditional look a "twist," as the designer, Daniel Parke, describes it. Behind the crystal chandeliers and Georgian furniture there is what he calls "a certain edited, tailored approach" that typifies the Donghia design philosophy even in this context.

"The clients wanted English traditional — very much in keeping with the taste of the times — but they came to us because they were fans of Donghia furniture design," Parke explains. "They wanted a new approach to English traditional."

And they got it, in architecture that was redefined in bold strokes to give the rooms a formal balance, and in colors and materials that bring the eighteenth century into the twentieth. In the master bedroom, for example, a Georgian chair wears khaki-colored satin, and the walls are upholstered in mohair. In general the colors tend to be "grayed-out and muted," says the designer.

"We hadn't done English or French rooms before. Donghia's style was contemporary, and we've continued his design precepts, so we tried to be a little offbeat with this English traditional — it's not layered or all 'chintzed up.'"

Parke says he has long shared the late designer's outlook and his affinity for the luxurious simplicity advocated by Jean-Michel Frank. Born in Wisconsin, Parke was associated with two other design firms after graduating from the Fashion Institute of Technology, but when he saw Donghia's work, "it clicked," he says. "I was strongly attracted by everything he stood for in design."

Parke says that he prefers to work in slightly overscale dimensions, as did Donghia. For a more typical client, though, with a typically small and architecturally undistinguished apartment, he eschewed the usual inclination to make the rooms look larger and instead played up the coziness of the space. However, this is coziness defined in terms of sleekness and sophistication. The colors are subdued but rich, and sensual textures are subtly interplayed, with leather, sisal, mohair, mirrors, and lacquer juxtaposed under a ceiling of silver tea paper. The windows are occluded; this is definitely a *nighttime* apartment, for a young woman executive, an art dealer for whom the "traditional" Donghia look is contemporary. □

For a master bedroom designed around Georgian antiques, Parke upholstered the walls in mohair and used khaki-colored satin on an armchair to add a typical Donghia touch. On the burl tall chest are sang-de-boeuf porcelains from the Qianlong period (1736–1795).

Opposite: Parke completely reworked the architecture in this East Side duplex to create the right formal background for the traditional English atmosphere the clients wanted. The lacquered Chinese coat and hat cupboards are from the eighteenth century, as is the English tea table with a pierced gallery. The painting over the fireplace is by an American artist, Frederick Carl Frieseke.

An itinerant "cast of characters"

RICHARD GIGLIO

Decorating is really just another art form, believes painter Richard Giglio, who says that *his* art is "about New York." So too is Giglio's life- and home-style: energetic, everchanging, highly eclectic. For him decorating is also a completely natural talent that he goes at with both hands, simultaneously.

"I'm ambidextrous and dyslexic," he says as though confiding a mischievous secret. "That's why I'm so highly visual. I see something once, and it's emblazoned on my brain." He works fast, consequently, and then moves on, never lingering more than three days on a painting — "If it takes longer than that," he says, "it usually ends up in the garbage!" — and seldom staying longer than a year or two in any apartment. There have been some sixteen different ones since his student days at Pratt Institute, and they have taken him from the luxury of an Upper East Side duplex in a town house owned by the designer Angelo Donghia (who lived on the two lower floors) to a heatless SoHo loft ("before SoHo *was*"), and now to a tiny penthouse on the high West Side of town, overlooking the Hudson River and New Jersey beyond.

Not that home is a matter of easy-come, easy-go for Giglio. Although he says he has a "time thing — I'm a Gemini and I like to keep moving," he always retains what he calls his "cast of characters": three favorite antique chairs that remind him of people, a tall African mask acquired in Amsterdam, and two silver-leafed plaster torchères from Syrie Maugham's shop, copied after Giacometti's design for Jean-Michel Frank.

Before he settled his "cast" on the West Side, he claims to have looked at eighty-seven different

Opposite: Richard Giglio's apartments, like his paintings, are ever-changing, always evolving. When he lived and worked at the top of Angelo Donghia's town house, the scene included one of Isamu Noguchi's lamps, some plaster masks, and Giglio's own drawings.

Right: The artist's duplex on the top floors of Donghia's house had been "wallpapered, fabricked, ruched . . . all in red" when he first lived there. He revised it in white, retaining such favorite objects as a Louis XVI chair, another small French chair, a cement cachepot made by his grandfather, and a painting that turned out *not* to be by Claude Lorrain. (Photographs by Angelo Donghia)

apartments. "This one was hands down the ugliest. And smallest, too, just twenty-three by eleven feet. But what it had was a situation that allows total privacy. . . . I come up the stairs to the fifteenth floor, and I'm at the top of the world, alone over the city. It's surreal."

Add to that Giglio's determination to live in an "atelier — all artists must have an atelier," and his penchant for open spaces: he dislikes furniture shoved against walls; he loves seeing people sitting around a table, especially if that table is in the kitchen. "This entire apartment is a kitchen!" he exclaims.

So it is that guests at the "cabin" are always in the kitchen, now an ell of white counters and appliances that edges the entry and flows into the bright all-in-one room. Giglio carved the open space from a former "3½ rm apt w/riv view," wrapping a large deck around three exterior sides, over what had been a tar roof. He also punched as many windows as he could through the walls, including a skylight over the kitchen area and a round "porthole" beside his huge daybed to make him feel "like I'm on a ship."

It was windows of another kind that originally led the artist into interior design. His Pratt B.F.A. in hand, Giglio started his career by designing window displays for stylish stores along Fifth Avenue. He was in good company, he now says with a laugh: "Warhol, Jasper Johns, Rosenquist, Rauschenberg — we all did windows!" From Fifth Avenue he moved to Madison Avenue, to commercial art and fashion illustration. And from there, he says, "It was a totally natural step to interior design."

"A room is a space, as a piece of paper is a space. I've never thought about interior design in terms of a living room, or piece of furniture. It's an art. And art is about an idea. When I look at a blank paper, it tells me what to do.

"So does an empty room."   □

Because Giglio believes that "everyone loves to sit in the kitchen," his is open to the rest of the space. Still lifes of fresh fruits and vegetables are a favorite decorative accessory, and "you can eat them, too."

Opposite: The artist's "old friends" regrouped in "the cabin's" single room. When he redesigned the West Side penthouse, Giglio punched new windows of different shapes through the walls, including the "porthole" over his sofa-cum-bed.

Making the "big-time" gesture

JEFF BILHUBER
TOM SCHEERER

Jeff Bilhuber sees New York as a "masculine town, diverse, bold, dynamic — the Big Time. Things are always churning, working, moving in New York," he says. "It's the boardroom. Paris, on the other hand, is the bedroom. Paris is feminine. Women are blissfully happy there.

"Manhattan Style is masculine, protective, so women feel good here, too, but it's a city of neutrals and primary colors. The urban landscape can't take pastels."

Bilhuber's partner, Tom Scheerer, nods his assent. In the five years since they founded Bilhuber, Incorporated, the firm has become known for work based on strong architectural backgrounds, a palette of mostly neutral colors, and very little of what Bilhuber calls "fluff."

"If the room has integrity, character, and personality on its own, you need fewer frills to distract the eye," he maintains.

There are few frills indeed in the Bilhuber, Incorporated, idiom. Scheerer is an architect, a graduate of Cooper Union; Bilhuber holds a degree in hotel administration from Cornell and had already worked his way through several creative careers — painter and sculptor, actor, and television producer — before he turned to interior design. His first assignments were for commercial spaces, but he says, "I could only do so much with flame-retardant fabrics!"

Although they converged from different perspectives, the designers agree that they have always been close in their design ideas: "Tom thought architecture should be more decorative, and I thought decorating should be more architectural," Bilhuber points out.

Their philosophies dovetail in a look they describe as "Modernist American. We make no effort to re-create another time or place or country," Scheerer emphasizes. "We're New York designers, and we like what we see in New York."

When it comes to clients' apartments, however, they say they see too much sameness and impersonal space, along with characterless architecture, low ceilings, and confused floor plans. A top priority for the team is to reconfigure, dramatize, and open up space to achieve good scale and proportion. In an old apartment on Central Park West, for example, they reorganized a lineup of rooms, pulling bedroom space into the sitting room and carving out an entirely new entry that adds a sense of arrival.

Across town, in a postwar apartment with low ceilings and less personality, they built walls and widened and opened doorways right up to the ceiling to give the rooms added strength. Here, too, they created an entry hall — now darkly mirrored and dramatic — by sacrificing eight feet of living-room space. Designed for a Japanese economist who came to the city with only a suitcase, the space is tightly edited yet comfortable, serene in the Eastern sense yet masculine, very New York.

Bilhuber, Incorporated, designs furnishings as well as interiors ("Otherwise we'd just be shopping companions to our clients"). Their style is what Bilhuber calls "familiar modern": "The materials and ideas are familiar, but the interpretation is ours." As translated by one of the string of craftspeople they have cultivated across the country, their "familiar modern" attitude distinguishes a bleached walnut table that the partners say is a "distillation of historic styles." It shows up again in a floor painted to resemble tortoiseshell — "We've gotten bored with realistic faux finishes; we think they should be more playful." In their hands, even ordinary striped walls have a new twist: wide stripes of matte-finish paint alternate with stripes painted in glossy lacquer. It's a matter of, as Bilhuber says, "taking a familiar idea and giving it a kick in the pants!" □

Bilhuber, Incorporated, created a new entrance for an apartment on Central Park West by stealing eight feet of space from the living room. The design team enriched the floor with faux tortoiseshell and put copper mirrors on the walls. The eighteenth-century Venetian tole chandelier, hanging over a bleached walnut table of Bilhuber's design, is beaded with uncut rock crystals.

To enhance the sense of "shimmering light" in the apartment, Jeff Bilhuber and Tom Scheerer bleached the floors and covered the walls with Indian bark paper, made in New Mexico and applied in squares. They also stripped and bleached the late-eighteenth-century Irish tall table, which stands under a Directoire mirror.

Opposite: The Bilhuber team's "familiar modern" approach: Louis XVI chairs in black leather surround an extension table of bleached ash. They reinterpreted yet another traditional motif for the console covered in lacquered parchment. One of a pair of portraits by Robert Longo hangs beside the accordian-shaded window.

Crescent-topped Italian fruitwood chairs from the early nineteenth century surround an adjustable Japanese ratcheted table in the dining area of a once-bland postwar apartment. Bilhuber, Incorporated, added a new wall to balance the new doorway into the study. The drawing is by Luis Frangella.

Opposite: The apartment's low ceilings called for a strong vertical element; the designers supplied it by opening up the wall to what was once a second bedroom — now the study. The collage/painting over the sofa is by Doug Craft; the paper Moravian stars are a Bilhuber signature.

A 50 percent solution

CARL STEELE

An interior designer who is also serious about fine art, Carl Steele needs two homes in which to hang those hats. One is a center-city town house in his native Philadelphia; the other, an East Side apartment in Manhattan, is deliberately sophisticated and energized with contemporary art: "When in Rome . . . ," Steele reflects, smiling.

He spends at least 50 percent of his time "in Rome," on behalf of clients in both cities and for his own research and entertainment. Manhattan is also where he does most of his shopping for art. A graduate of the Philadelphia College of Art, Steele believes that good art is much more than a decorative accessory, so his thirty-year-old design firm, Carl Steele Associates, Incorporated, carries an unusually large inventory of artworks.

In New York, Steele practices what he preaches: his apartment is centered around a diverse collection of fine and decorative arts, focusing on the twentieth century. Included are a print by Frank Stella, paintings by Elaine Kurtz and Joel Perlstein, and bronze furniture by Diego Giacometti, bought directly from the artist in Paris.

"Giacometti was quite sophisticated, very different out for dinner than in the studio. He was even wearing a cape," relates Steele, who came away from Paris with four bronze armchairs, a cocktail table, and a lamp. He bought the collection at what he remembers as "reasonable prices, even though Giacometti was very aware that his furniture was being highly collected."

Also collected in Paris were the rotund fauteuil that Steele sees as a "cartoon of a French chair," from David Hicks's studio, and a reproduction Jean-Michel Frank leather-skirted chair that now sits before the fireplace, next to a round French Empire table. The arrangement attests to the practical design approach Steele employed when he created the smallish apartment that had to serve also as his New York office. The table, for example, works both for dining and, between meals, as a desk. In the bedroom, he "floats" the bed away from the wall to enhance the illusion of space, and partners it with antique Chinese chairs that are used as bedside tables. The tiny entrance hall does double duty as a gallery for more art, set off from the sitting room and softened with two-sided, tied-back portieres. Even the eighteenth-century Chinese panels, since incorporated into doors, have been hung on the wall as *objets d'art*.

"I'm a great believer in flexibility — and in comfort," says the designer. He points out that the sitting room, abundant with sofas, chairs, light sources, and conveniently placed tables, is calculated to serve many functions, as he uses it for work, for entertaining, and for relaxing after a day with clients in New York showrooms and galleries.

"I spend as much time in the galleries as I do in the market shopping for other furnishings. If clients are not already collectors, I try to introduce them to art.

"But," he emphasizes, "art is not just part of the overall theme.

"It's much more important than that." □

Steele acquired the Giacometti table from the artist himself. Above it are a print by Frank Stella, some eighteenth-century Chinese panels, and *(at right)* a painting by Elaine Kurtz.

An antique Chinese chair serves as a
table beside the bed, which has been allowed
to "float" free of the walls to make the room
look more spacious. Above it is a
"blackboard" painting of football plays by
Bill Richards.

Opposite: A pair of bronze chairs by
Giacometti flank the fireplace in the sitting
room, set off by portieres from the art-filled
entry hall. The leather-skirted chair at the
dining-cum-work table came from Paris and
was based on a design by Jean-Michel Frank.

A taste for color that has matured to "non-color" imparts harmony to a sitting room enriched with antiques and art from many different periods and places. Paintings by two women working a century apart — Rosa Bonheur (*over the sofa*) and Helen Frankenthaler — coexist handsomely with an eighteenth-century Chinese silver-leaf table, a Chinese bronze deer, and a Japanese high-relief bowl from the nineteenth century.

Far from city sounds and colors

J. HYDE CRAWFORD

The flowers came first, and early in J. Crawford's career. As the creative force behind Bonwit Teller's high-fashion ads for some twenty-five years, he designed the famous nosegay of violets on the store's shopping bags, soon recognized the world over.

But flowers no longer hold Crawford's interest now that he has turned his talents to Quadrille, the designer wallpaper and fabric house that he started with partners some two decades ago and of which he remains president. Certainly there are few florals and not a hint of chintz on any of the three floors in his elegant 1868 town house. Here the emphasis is on what the designer calls "the richer palette of texture and non-colors" with which he has fashioned his "oasis" in the city. "Sound-wise and color-wise, this house is so far removed from New York," he says. The upholstered walls in the front bedroom and the private, tree-filled back garden are only partly responsible for the quiet that pervades indoors. It is the quiet of another era altogether, of other countries. Yet overall there is a definite sense of time — *now* — and place — *New York* — that emanates largely from Crawford's art collection, most of it American abstracts from the 1960s and '70s. The art energizes the rooms, filled with well-patinaed, mostly European and Oriental antiques, without overpowering them. It is the sure hand of a connoisseur with a stone sense of scale and color that can give a Helen Frankenthaler top billing in a sitting room that also contains an eighteenth-century Chinese table, an Italian crystal chandelier, and an Aubusson rug. The "non-colors," in both the room and the art, make it all work handsomely.

"When you are young, you want to be radical," the Parsons-trained designer observes. "Now the palette that pleases me has more to do with textures, and with the colors of marbles, bronzes, and other metals." The sitting-room walls are mottled a metallic gray up to the double surprise of wide moldings picked out in warm colors and a ceiling covered in trompe l'oeil paper by Quadrille. Bright with sunlight by day — a rarity in a city where skyscrapers cast long shadows — the room also "glows" at night, the designer reports. "*Oasis* is the perfect word for the house, I think," he says.

Other words come to mind as well: classic, comfortable, timeless, touched occasionally with whimsy — such as the antelope-spotted rug in the hallway or the Italian faux marble chest in the dining room. But no flowers. The Virginia-born designer smiles and explains, "I'm trying to stay away from flowers. The world has already seen too much chintz." □

In his own bedroom, the designer covers a French
Empire bed with an American quilt and glazes the walls
with bronze mirrors. The painting between the windows is
Napoleon Bidding Farewell to Egypt, by Gérôme.

Opposite: The small hallway makes a big statement about
Crawford's sure way with scale and color. The desk and
double-gourd bottle are Chinese; the Quadrille fabric on
the eighteenth-century Italian chair plays back the colors in
the painting by Richard Diebenkorn.

The walls in the street-level kitchen are made
of barnboard stained gunmetal-dark
to serve as background for the light-colored
furniture. The nineteenth-century faux marble
chest is Italian; eighteenth-century painted
Scandinavian chairs surround an old
pine table centered with a terra-cotta
garden ornament.

"Making the right connections"

KEVIN McNAMARA

Kevin McNamara has said that he believes in the "democracy of taste," in juxtaposing true collector's pieces with things of humble origin, so long as the effect pleases his eye or appeals to his sense of humor.

Indeed, the designer has painted over ordinary cheesecloth to achieve the richly textured walls in his own apartment. There, too, a simple wicker basket filled with pine cones may sit under a Louis XV table with delicate gilt feet.

The point, according to the designer, is not how rare or expensive an object is, but whether one can "make the right connections" with it. Consequently, McNamara says that he is open equally to junk-shop discoveries and to signed pieces of court furniture. But whatever their provenance, the designer's finds meld congenially in the colorful and lush traditional rooms that have become his signature. Almost invariably, the rooms will have a French accent, in his personal reinterpretation of the traditional look he became

conversant with at both McMillen, Incorporated, and Parish-Hadley Associates. A graduate of Boston University, McNamara was the first exception to Mrs. Brown's dictum against hiring any designer who had not been trained at Parsons (though eventually he did study there).

Since McNamara formed his namesake company in the early 1970s, classic traditional design and a strong sense of architecture have been the backbone of his work. He is also known for the clear, singing colors with which he fast-forwards traditional rooms to meet the demands of life in the 1990s. In the process, he usually skips the nineteenth century altogether: "Kevin is always fighting past the nineteenth century to get back to the purity of the eighteenth," observes a colleague.

The twentieth century is another thing entirely. For a client with a collection of modern art, McNamara managed a smooth blend of *then* and *now* — of classic antiques and works by the likes

Opposite: In his own apartment, McNamara painted over cheesecloth to give texture to the walls. A Venetian mirror reflects a view of the East River; the garniture below it was an early purchase by "a starving designer," McNamara says. The small drawing on the Louis XV table is by Henry Moore.

Right: A mirrored wall opposite the fireplace reflects an arrangement of delftware on the demilune Louis XVI *console à dessert.* The flanking Louis XVI chairs are from a set of four.

of Léger, Dubuffet, and Frankenthaler — never sublimating one to the other. It is a skillful update of what Elsie de Wolfe did so well — and so startlingly, at the time — when she paired eighteenth-century antiques with contemporary artwork.

In the same apartment, McNamara has done Elsie one better, designing eighteenth-century antiques using leading-edge technology. The client wanted a king-size tester bed, nonexistent in the Sheraton style that McNamara had in mind. Xerography to the rescue: the design team simply photocopied elements from Sheraton's *Cabinet-Maker and Upholster's Drawing Book*, of 1791, adjusting and enlarging to the required size, "just as any cabinetmaker would have done in Sheraton's time."

McNamara must have had just this attitude in mind when he told an interviewer, "I think a room should always remain 'young.' By this I mean open to change, susceptible to new ideas."   □

McNamara used monochromes to create a calm background for a dramatic Léger tapestry in a client's entry hall. A Dubuffet hangs over the Empire console; the urns are from the eighteenth century.

Kevin McNamara used xerography to stretch a two-century-old design by Sheraton to the king-size dimensions requested by the client. The painting over the fireplace is by Milton Avery.

Opposite: In the living room, an enameled bronze relief by Léger hangs opposite an English chinoiserie mirror from the mid-1700s. On the far wall (*at left*) is a painting by Helen Frankenthaler. The blue brocade chairs are Régence, from a set of four; the rug is a late Savonnerie.

A collector's collection

GARRICK C. STEPHENSON

With literally the entire world of antiques to choose from, the renowned Manhattan antique dealer and collector Garrick Stephenson has gone about furnishing his own apartment with careful discernment, slowly and deliberately choosing what he personally wants to come home to.

The truth of the matter, Stephenson maintains, is that after almost four decades in the business, he buys only what pleases his personal taste anyway, whether he is shopping for his celebrated gallery or looking for a new old something to add to his private collection. "Antiques are too personal to buy what you don't like," he contends.

Stephenson's "look" is eloquently defined in his own apartment. Drawn from various centuries and continents to create an eclectic blend, his personal choices have imparted a stately *presence* to a once-ordinary space in the upper East Seventies. When he moved here a half decade or so ago, Stephenson was greeted by unattractive plain walls and bookcases of dubious architectural ancestry. A trained designer who went through the Parsons School after taking a liberal arts degree at Yale and then worked with the firm of McMillen, Incorporated, Stephenson first solved the problem posed by the bland background. To center the elongated living room, he created a faux fireplace with an Empire chimneypiece from the late eighteenth or early nineteenth century. Then he added columns and imposing ceiling-high pediments to the pedestrian inset bookcases. Angled *faux bois* walls, defined with darker mouldings, now offer a warm, congruous setting for a formally balanced gathering of mainly French pieces.

Accessories are as multifarious as one would expect from a collector who travels five months of every year, gleaning the excellent and the unusual from Europe and Scandinavia.

"I do love to buy," Stephenson confirms. "And it's fun to sell . . . so I can go buy more." □

Opposite: The renowned collector's "menagerie" includes a wry cat–cum–bird feeder by Giacometti and a pair of marble dromedaries, possibly eighteenth-century French, displayed on a pair of gilt French consoles dating from 1795. The gold matchbox is by Fabergé.

Right: Swan bergères, circa 1805–1810, flank an Empire chimneypiece in the vintage sitting room that Garrick Stephenson has imposed upon an "ordinary" apartment. He also added the *faux bois* walls and the impressive bookcase pediments.

The past, revisited and refreshed

MARK HAMPTON

Artist, author, and designer of furniture and fabrics as well as interiors, Mark Hampton could be called a Renaissance man, except that the era he specializes in came later, around the eighteenth century — the Age of Enlightenment.

Hampton's focus, actually, is more English than French, more American than English — aside from his affinity for London tailors — and, in the final analysis, more New York than anything else, in spite of the fact that he has become known as the "White House Decorator" for all his work in Washington. Hampton has renovated the private quarters of the White House as well as its West Wing, Blair House, Camp David, and the Bush family home in Kennebunkport, Maine.

But then, he has also refurbished Gracie Mansion, the official residence of the mayor of New York, and designed interiors for the Metropolitan Museum of Art and the landmark Carlyle Hotel.

If work on such highly visible historic sites requires a large measure of authenticity based on scholarly research, Hampton brings that to bear — and more. He is known for his "refreshed recreations of the eighteenth-century spirit," as one design historian put it. In Hampton's hands, even historic rooms feel comfortable and *contemporary*. He is a classicist who earned a Master of Fine Arts degree (at New York University's Institute of Fine Arts) and understands both the art of good living and the decorator's role in it: balancing "the need for beauty, chic, and glamour with the more prosaic needs of domesticity in the same room."

Hampton's early training was well suited to that goal. Born in Indiana, he started his design career in association with David Hicks, the English decorator widely celebrated for his unorthodox — and most unstodgy — approach to traditional interiors. Hicks started a revolution of sorts in the 1960s with his small-geometric-patterned carpets, and Hampton, who also attended the London School of Economics, served as his American representative in New York. That association, moreover, took Hampton into many of the grand old homes of England.

It is no surprise that Hampton worked next with Mrs. Henry Parish II and then as an associate of McMillen, Incorporated. Both design firms are known for having a sure hand with elegant, updated traditional interiors. When Hampton decided to start his own practice, in 1976, he had the new traditionalism firmly in his well-tailored pocket.

Since that time he has been credited as a major force behind the resurgence of traditionalism on a national scale, and possibly beyond. Certainly his clients move in international circles — clients such as Estée Lauder, Rupert Murdoch, and the Carter Burdens. Hampton has also taken his very American style abroad — to, among other places, the American Academy in Rome.

When he comes home to Park Avenue, the setting he has created for his own family life has been gleaned, predictably, from many countries and time periods, all orchestrated into a gracious apartment filled with faux finishes, classical references, and warmth. The "beauty, chic, and glamour" Hampton says he strives for are there, but the overall feeling of comfortable domesticity is anything but "prosaic." □

A mid-nineteenth-century Gothic stool sits before the fireplace between the Victorian slipper chairs. Hampton cut the eglomise mirror to fit over the chimneypiece. The ivory model of a ruin is a nineteenth-century Indian carving.

Opposite: The eighteenth and nineteenth centuries meld seamlessly in Mark Hampton's sitting room, where a quartet of Louis XVI chairs share the same fabric with a pair of Victorian slipper chairs from the 1840s. The eglomise mirror is one of a pair; the trompe l'oeil paintings beside it are French, from the early eighteenth century.

Eighteen framed illustrations from Pyne's *Royal Residences*, published in the 1790s, line the walls in Hampton's dining room. The William IV Gothic Revival chairs flank a white gesso table in the William Kent style, over which hangs a Venetian mirror. The Regency console is one of a pair, and the carpet is by David Hicks.

T. KELLER DONOVAN

In his new order of things, Keller Donovan says he has discovered symmetry. For a while there, the process of building his own design firm turned him into the "shoemaker's child," claims the popular young designer: his own living space remained somewhat "barefoot" while he concentrated on beautifying the lives of his clients.

"Now I want order in my own life, everything in pairs, and in a traditional setting." The new order is continually evolving in Donovan's West End Avenue apartment. From the foyer forward, a kind of formal balance prevails in a setting that is traditional in feeling, right down to what is essentially a red, white, and blue color scheme. But this is *upbeat* traditional, fresh and clean, its two-by-two formal balance here and there offset by objects of singular interest. Occasionally, too, there are pieces left over "from my former life," as Donovan says, such as the paired white wicker étagères that flank the sofa, itself reclaimed from a designer show house for which he created a room.

He also puts a fresh spin on the red, white, and blue color scheme, translating it into watermelon red, gray-white, and the bright blueberry of the sofa. The walls are the softest gray, framed within white mouldings, and red pops up at its most extroverted on the grass-cloth-covered foyer wall. There, track lights have been dropped a foot or so below the ceiling to illuminate Donovan's favorite "vignette": twenty framed rectangles of ribbon-like colors over a table that bears his moniker, or something very close to it. Carved decisively into the apron of the vintage Irish pub table are the initials "T.K.," preceded by "T. Kelly." Donovan was known as T.K. in college, he says, "So when I saw that table in a store window, I had to have it."

The ribbons of color framed above the table were patterns that denoted the rank and provenance of Japanese samurai. Donovan found them in a bookshop in England, had them glass-framed in Paris, and hand-carried them back to New York.

Other such personal touches illuminate the apartment: the fabric he bought in India for a dollar a yard to cover cushions on the dining banquette; his collection of wicker-wrapped flasks and condiment holders from Victorian picnic baskets; the simple ceramic pots that he painted white and turned into lamps for the bedroom. In here the mood turns light and countrylike. Blue and white prevail; any accent color comes from the neutrals of the sisal carpet and the basket collection, including the sweet-grass baskets he commissioned from artisans in Charleston, South Carolina. A ceiling fan hums overhead between white beams that Donovan says remind him of the whitewashed roofs in Bermuda. But the "headboard" on the bed confirms that this is still New York City, where every square inch of living space must work: the designer has stacked years' worth of decorating magazines wall-to-wall, creating a graphic design that is as handsome as it is practical.

Donovan clearly enjoys such small flights of fancy, one reason, he says, that he became a designer and not the architect he imagined himself as when he was growing up in Short Hills, New Jersey. Another reason was his stint as fashion coordinator of furniture at Bloomingdale's, a job that stimulated him to enroll in night courses at the Parsons School and eventually led to the launch of T. Keller Donovan, Incorporated, in 1977.

"Design *is* ideas," he believes. "I enjoy coming up with new ideas, new interests. For example, I never liked symmetry; now I want two of everything. At this point, I know how I want to live: with wonderful things culled from everywhere in the world — in a traditional setting." ☐

Glass-framed prints of samurai epaulets are hung in formation over Donovan's initialed Irish pub table. He bought the "Anglo-Egyptian" Chippendale chair *(at left of doorway)* from a London dealer. The English tartanware on the dining table is part of a collection.

Opposite: Updated traditional: Keller Donovan's West Side sitting room is "evolving" around a grayed-white, red, and blue color scheme. Audubon prints and baskets are a recurring theme in the apartment.

The nineteenth-century ship's model was made in Scandinavia; the bottle, dishes, and bowl are Japanese, dating from the twentieth century.

The antique rocking horse on the bedside table
dates from the early 1800s; Donovan bought it from the
apartment's previous owners. The sweet-grass baskets are
from Charleston; the painting came as a Christmas card
from the artist Brad Winslow.

Opposite: Country in the city: Donovan's blue and white
bedroom features a wall-to-wall "headboard" of
interior-design magazines.

MARIETTE HIMES GOMEZ

It doesn't take much to please Mariette Himes Gomez, as long as she is working with the very best. Her approach to designing interiors, for herself and for her clients, she says, is "to use a few very good pieces" within a context of contemporary design. She believes in simplifying architecture, not only to enrich the process of living, but also to create noncompetitive backgrounds for those "very good pieces."

"It's not important whether they're eighteenth-century English antiques or primitives," according to Ms. Gomez, "as long as they are among the best of the period."

Hers is a practiced eye when it comes to discerning the best. She studied interior design and fine arts at the Rhode Island School of Design and then took a degree in fine arts from the New York School of Interior Design. Before starting her own firm, Gomez Associates, Incorporated, she worked in the design offices of Parish-Hadley and of the architect Edward Durrell Stone.

Art, antiques, and handcrafts are of the essence in Ms. Gomez's work. But even as she is creating a background for a collection, her rooms manage to function comfortably as well. Moreover, the hand of the designer seldom shows: the architecture is never contrived; the window treatments tend to be unobtrusive; the furniture arrangements are dictated by pure logic. However, Gomez-followers — and there are many, especially among the design media — can identify her work at a glance. There are two giveaways: her

trademark combination of blue and green and her fondness for circles.

Both themes are evident in the town house that she shares with her architect husband, Raymond, and their two teenage children. Here two additional factors exerted an influence on the design. The Gomezes entertain often, in a not-large space, so she has wrapped the sitting room on three sides with a sectional sofa that can seat up to fourteen people. Behind it, displayed on narrow shelving that parallels the seating unit all around, is the couple's extensive collection of pre-Columbian pottery. Acquired when they lived in Peru during the building of a hotel he designed, the collection demanded display space.

A few other "good things," notably drawings and paintings, are also propped on the shelf to lean against the white-painted brick wall. By night, track lights give the room a gallery atmosphere. Ceiling-mounted all around, they wash over the richly textured wall and dramatize the Gomezes' collections. Continuing throughout the apartment, the white brick serves as background for a disparate assemblage of antiques and art. An eighteenth-century Spanish bed with an ornately carved headboard wears an American quilt of blue and white circles; on top is a small pillow made from an Aubusson tapestry. The chair that pulls up to a Danish desk beside the bed is French Empire; on the other side is a wall-hung cabinet dating from the 1900s. American-made and unassuming, it is painted blue-green — "My ultimates," Ms. Gomez confirms, smiling. □

The circle motifs that Mariette Himes Gomez delights in show up above the fireplace in her town-house living room, where a large collection, including pre-Columbian Peruvian pottery, is on perpetual display.

The disparate assemblage of antiques in the
Gomezes' bedroom includes a painted Spanish bed from
the eighteenth century, an American quilt, and a French
Empire chair.

Opposite: To make space in her own town house, Ms.
Gomez framed three sides of the sitting room with a seating
unit and backed it with a display shelf for the couple's
collection of pre-Columbian pottery. The pencil drawings
on the far wall are by Jack Tworkov; the chairs drawn up to
the grain-painted table are eighteenth-century Italian.

An intimate dining area in a client's kitchen features a painted red American table with a candlestand base. The tiny pictures are framed Shaker seed bags.

Below: A nineteenth-century pine harvest table is surrounded by handmade Windsor chairs in the dining room. Next to the sponge-painted cupboard (from New Hampshire) are a contemporary sculpture by John Okulick and a painting by Ben Schonzeit. The horse weather vane is full-bodied; the rug, an antique Heriz.

In a client's Fifth Avenue apartment, Mariette Himes Gomez
simplifies backgrounds to emphasize a collection of American
furniture and artworks. An eighteenth-century Queen Anne
highboy, made in Rhode Island, dominates the living room. The
tea table is early-eighteenth-century, from Newport. Both the
blanket chest beside the sofa and the full-bodied fish weather
vane in the window came from Pennsylvania.

135

"A few good things" from different slices of
time: a French Art Nouveau cane chair, a child's
wooden bicycle from the early 1900s, and a bronze
sculpture by John Okulick.

Opposite: For an art-gallery owner, her lawyer husband,
and their kindergarten child, Ms. Gomez orchestrated a
juxtaposition of contemporary art and rustic furniture,
including a pair of late-nineteenth-century Scandinavian
benches, a cocktail table by Dave Nyzio, and stenciled
Hitchcock chairs upstairs on the dining level.

"An accumulation of things"

MELVIN DWORK

Never mind that his client roster reads like a Fortune 100 list, or that he numbers both European nobility and luminaries from the American theater and film industries among those whose rooms he has designed. When it comes to his own home, Mel Dwork says he does not decorate, he *accumulates*, gradually acquiring art, furniture, and artifacts that are "consistent with my look." His apartment on the edge of SoHo, a single-bedroom duplex in a recently rehabilitated older building, represents "years and years of accumulations, mostly from friends," Dwork says, surveying the space.

Among those gifts from friends is the old wooden skid that Dwork uses as a cocktail table. The artist Frank Faulkner found it on a SoHo street, painted the primitive motifs, and gave it to the designer. Rough-hewn and *real*, the skid fits in easily with the room's other primitives, both the old — the African stools, ceremonial masks, and carvings and the pre-Columbian pottery — and the new — the linear metal sculpture by Bruno Romeda, a contemporary Italian artist.

Over all of this, like a soaring green sculpture, a large banana tree raises its leaves to the light of the window that extends to the double height of the room. Dwork reworked the apartment space dramatically before he moved in, adding storage cabinets around the lower walls, taking away an overwrought fireplace, sealing an entry into the kitchen, and opening up more space by adding a spiral stair in place of the angled steps that formerly led to the upper level.

"It's taken me awhile to get it right," he says of the three-year decorating process. "I'm not a typical decorator — that is, I don't think 'decorating' day and night, and I don't redo my own rooms. I like to come home and just *live* in them."

There are, however, certain things that Dwork insists on living with, and some that he adamantly opposes. Take chairs, for example: "I have a passion for chairs," he says, and they are indeed imposing, the oversized pair facing into the seating area of the room. One is French, Louis Quatorze, from the late sixteenth century, covered in rich old needlepoint; the other is seventeenth-century Flemish, done in tooled Spanish leather. A Chinese bamboo chair from the eighteenth century reclines elegantly against the wall beside the tightly upholstered bed. On the other side is a low, primitive African stool. And upstairs, in what Dwork calls his "winter bedroom," an eighteenth-century needlepoint-covered French chair shares space with a wooden chair from nineteenth-century America, flat-backed in design and primitive in execution.

Dwork also favors the primitive in art — "It's very sophisticated," he says — and has made rich antique fabrics his trademark, buying fragments and making them into pillows for himself as well as for clients.

What does not find favor with the Parsons-trained designer is formal dining rooms. Despite his fondness for chairs, Dwork says he prefers eating informally, away from the usual table-chair arrangement. He also likes to "put a little kick" in clients' lives by providing them with banquette seating, at least along one side of the dining table.

This is a realistic solution for all-too-often space-shy city apartments, and being realistic appeals to the Missouri-born Dwork, who graduated from the Art Institute in his native Kansas City before coming to New York and Parsons.

"My last apartment had been in a large penthouse on the Upper West Side. Wonderful apartment, nice neighborhood, but *this*," he says, surveying the roofs, water tanks, and fire escapes that form the view through his single large window, "this is real." □

The banana palm has moved from apartment to apartment like a favorite piece of sculpture. It towers over Dwork's tightly upholstered "summer" bed, with its antique-fabric pillows. The trunk is eighteenth-century Japanese, made of lacquered leather. The stool and the baboon head (there is a real skull inside) are African.

Left: No fan of formal dining rooms, Dwork instead sets up his Louis XVI table in the well of his spiral staircase and pulls the large sixteenth- and seventeenth-century chairs in from the living room. The sculpture is from his collection of primitives from several continents.

Opposite: The view down the spiral stair that Mel Dwork added to his SoHo duplex: the grand armchairs are sixteenth-century French (*at left*) and Flemish, dating from the seventeenth century. Dwork designed the upholstered pieces facing each other across the wooden-skid cocktail table.

Below: The "winter bedroom" on the second level is cozy, with black-green lacquered walls and a studded bed of Dwork's own design. The eighteenth-century pastels came home with the designer from his first trip to Paris. The straightforward primitive wooden chair is American, from the nineteenth century.

A late-seventeenth-century Dutch kas dominates the bedroom of a client's uptown pied-à-terre. Of black lacquer with brass mounts, it holds Javanese stacked baskets. A Giacometti-style bronze lamp illuminates the other artworks in the room: a David Hockney drawing, a fragment of medieval sculpture, and a Louis XIII stool.

Opposite: The dining banquette — a Dwork signature — is backed by a Japanese lacquer screen and a pair of Spanish iron candlesticks. Dwork updated the design of a Chinese trestle table for the dining table; the chairs are Louis XIII, from the late seventeenth century. In the foreground is a bronze stela by the Italian sculptor Bruno Romeda.

Symmetry, fantasy, scale

TOM BRITT

Against architectural backgrounds that must be "absolutely correct," designer Tom Britt orchestrates the unexpected into rooms that are as calm, classic, and timeless as they are highly personalized.

Whichever you encounter first, Britt himself or his interiors, the other will come as a surprise. The designer is the eye of a small hurricane, a telephone in each hand, it seems, prodding, checking, and organizing a dozen details of the several dozen projects that Thomas Britt, Incorporated, generally has in the works at many points around the globe. Energetic, urbane, and obviously enjoying it all immensely, the gravel-voiced Britt is very much the twentieth-century executive.

His rooms, however, are classic and calm, in the eighteenth-century tradition, oases of well-reasoned symmetry that are almost formal and altogether traceable to his strict classical training. Missouri-born, Britt took a degree in science from New York University and then went on to the Parsons School of Design, traveling to Paris to study, firsthand, the great classic interiors of Europe. But Britt's is a classicism overlaid with his own sense of the dramatic and the unexpected: tall bare branches soaring from a vase on a low table ("Better than a chandelier"); seventeenth-century Spanish baroque columns treated as freestanding sculpture in a client's living room; eighteenth-century Venetian atlantes supporting huge vases that tower over the corners of his own narrow dining room.

It is no surprise, then, to learn of Britt's great friendship with the eclectic decorator Rose Cumming. They met when he was twenty years old,

sent to her famed shop for a piece of fabric. "I was petrified; she was incredible, with her hair a brilliant purple and bright red lips, with pearls to her waist." The flamboyant Miss Cumming fueled Britt's penchant for drama on a grand scale, and since her death he has acquired several significant pieces that once belonged to her for his own collection. His office chair was hers, for example, and her unusual fabric-covered William and Mary table now resides in his drawing room, under a collection of bird prints that came from her "Forbidding Room" on Fifty-third Street (so called because it featured depictions of birds of prey, mice, snakes, and other pet eccentricities).

"The things I work with come from all over the world," Britt says. "I can never travel enough, never have too much exposure. My rooms are a flow of all these various influences. They show what's happening in the world *now*.

"But my work is also classic and timeless. You could put my rooms on a grid. They're very, very symmetrical, very calculated. Still, I never just re-create the past, and I'm fastidious about detail. The architectural background has to be absolutely correct, the way Jean-Michel Frank's rooms were based on architecture. You have to get the bones of it exactly right.

"Then what's wildly important is scale," he stresses. "Everything should be large, large enough to make a definitive statement. I like big accessories, and enough of them so they matter. When a room is ordered in the Classic manner, it creates an overall serenity and calmness. Even a small room can be grand — as in Pompeii — if the scale is right." □

With walls either mirrored or painted a deep aubergine, Britt's upstairs sitting room is formally balanced around a center table that sprouts flowering branches. Britt designed the ziggurat tables and the five-foot-deep sofa, which is covered in white Thai cotton. Flexible seating groups, he says, make this "a great party room at night, when the mirrors catch the light from the little lamps — there are eight of them, all alike."

Eighteenth-century Venetian atlantes bearing giant urns flank a Chippendale-style gilt mirror in Britt's dining room. Surrounded by Biedermeier chairs, the dining table is topped with tortoiseshell. On it is a collection of nineteenth-century Chinese altar accessories.

Opposite: Julius Caesar broods over an exotic arrangement of coral, shells, branches, and Swedish crystal on the chimneypiece in Britt's fin de siècle town-house apartment. He bleached the Louis XV Revival boiserie and the floor and covered all the upholstery in white Thai cotton to "simplify the room." Even the books on the twin pagodas of his design wear harmonizing pale glazed-paper wrappers.

Britt's sense of monumental scale adds drama to his design offices, where the walls are painted "stone" and great expanses of mirror stretch the space to infinity. The furnishings are laid out on a straight axis, with a porphyry bust of a Roman emperor on a stone pedestal in each niche. Surrounding the faux stone table are Italian Empire chairs upholstered in luggage leather. The tin lion mask is from London.

In one of the "grand gestures" he is so fond of, Tom Britt uses silk taffeta over the windows, imported architectural elements, and a stenciled border to conjure up an appropriate background for a client's collection of art and antiques. The baroque column is one of a pair from seventeenth-century Spain. The painting is by the seventeenth-century Dutch artist Abraham Janssens; the rug is an antique dhurrie.

Opposite: The unusual upholstered William and Mary table and the collection of bird prints in Britt's sitting room once belonged to his great friend the decorator Rose Cumming. He "crew-cut" the formerly bushy fringe on the table's edges and legs. The Chinese cachepots are from the Qianlong period.

A summation of taste

MAC II FOR BILL BLASS

Precisely because he has made his fame in the fast and ever-changing world of apparel fashion, designer Bill Blass goes home to a totally opposite environment. In the sepia stillness of a penthouse filled with the timeless, the classic, and the forever elegant, there is no mistaking that here lives a man of honed sensibilities, a man who could have it all but wants much more — the best, as defined by his highly personal taste.

His is an acquired taste, as Blass himself will tell you. The apartment was an entirely different thing during the first twenty years he lived there. Once there were high-fashion brown walls and a welter of collections, some of them good — his Oriental things, for example — and some just nice objects. For the apartment's latest incarnation, Blass edited them all out. Finally able to own what he had formerly been renting, the designer started bone-deep to create a fresh, lean habitat for himself. He turned, "for all the architectural and technical things," to his longtime friend Chessy Rayner, a partner, with Mica Ertegun, in the design firm Mac II. Together they are celebrated for their "architectural rigor" and their meticulous craftsmanship. Mac II applied both qualities to Blass's apartment, spending a year refining and redesigning the space. The gracious marble-floored foyer was expanded, the architecture was defined, and an open closet/dressing room was created between the master bedroom and bath.

"That was Chessy's idea," Blass says. "I've found that it's a good thing for a bachelor to have a lady decorator — she thinks of things I wouldn't, like turning that tiny bedroom into a big closet."

Through a glass serenely: a Louis XVI screen defines one end of the symmetrically balanced living room; a statue of Napoleon dominates the other. A large trompe l'oeil painting by the seventeenth-century Dutch painter Jacobus Biltius hangs over the late-eighteenth-century Irish side table. The column is a miniature of the one in the Place Vendôme.

Overall, Mac II's major contribution was to create a calm architectural background for the furniture, art, and *objets* that Blass finds pleasing enough to live with. It is an eclectic mix indeed, including drawings, paintings, sculpture, and furniture, gathered across countries, continents, and centuries. The furniture is both antique and newly custom-made, as seen in the twin living-room sofas upholstered in a neutral fabric by Mac II. These may be the lone twentieth-century addition, not counting fabrics (every one of them plain, save for the paisley on Blass's upholstered bed) and the sumptuous marble master bath ("You see Mica's hand there," Blass says).

Still, for all the old-world quality of the parts — the furnishings and art — the gestalt of the penthouse is *modern,* clean and spare. The architecture has been simplified, the arrangements are symmetrical and formal, and the walls are painted what Blass has called a "pale paper-bag color." Neutrality reigns, by careful design.

"I believe one needs monotone colors in one's home, a certain spareness. It's not good, living in color, in the city or in the country. I still have a red room in my country house" — he pulled out the scarlet Oriental chintz that once dominated the penthouse dining room — "and I'm going to change that, too."

Even the wondrously wide terrace that wraps around the apartment has been amended to suit Blass's desire for "a certain spareness." The elaborate plantings that once drew raves from the fashion press are no more. In their stead stand disciplined evergreens in tubs and a clear view toward the East River.

In sum, says Blass, the apartment "truly expresses my taste and what I believe. Nothing has been bought specifically to 'go' here. Everything is something I like. It is all my taste, all me." □

Flamboyant and rare, a Charles II cabinet is veneered in oyster-spotted lignum vitae. The arrangement above it attests to Blass's growing passion for classic motifs — sixteenth-century portrait medallions of ancient Romans, small paintings by Gérôme, and a Greek fragment dating from the first century B.C.

Opposite: Antique marble heads from Lord Pembroke's collection at Wilton stare out from the tops of Italian fluted mahogany columns in the dining room/library. Over the wall of mahogany bookcases arch brass library lights. The chairs are Swedish Empire, covered in off-white sailcloth.

The gallery continues in the open-closet dressing room that Mac II created from a small bedroom. A Biedermeier chest with faux ivory holds a collection of genuine old ivory *objets*. The painting, by Philpot, is of an unknown English officer in World War I.

Opposite: In the bedroom, the corner walls are given over to windows; the third wall holds part of Blass's collection of drawings and paintings, among them a Picasso as well as a magazine illustration by Remington.

DAVID ANTHONY EASTON

In a client's Fifth Avenue apartment, Easton moved walls to make way for a gallery on a grand manor-house scale, where the owner could display a collection of porcelain and books in lighted niches. The floors are marble; the columns and walls are faux marble.

David Anthony Easton spends much of his time in the eighteenth century. He gets there by jet. And when he returns to the twentieth century, he may have a real prize in hand — along with the antiques and authentic accoutrements he constantly seeks out for clients.

An architect as well as an interior designer, Easton has won several distinguished awards for the Georgian-style homes that he has designed and decorated in exacting detail, right down to the knobs on the doors and even, in at least one case, the sheets on the beds. He has, in his own words, a "passion" for what he does: taking a house from the initial sketches through construction and landscaping, all the way to the final ashtrays.

Easton has expressed his "constant amazement at the extremes, the time, effort, and money that people spend to create beauty." But if his clients are fanatical about authentic detail, the designer himself is no less so. Easton has been called "scholarly," and indeed, many of the most prestigious schools, museums, and historical associations in the country have invited him to lecture. He has also served on the faculty at Parsons, where he taught history of design for several years.

Easton characterizes himself as passionate, claiming, "Passion is what you need to be good, an unforgiving passion." His extends well beyond reproductions of Georgian houses, of course. Schooled in the classics, he may impart the lilt of eighteenth-century France to the drawing room of a client's Fifth Avenue apartment. Or create an octagonal fantasy of an entry by insetting the walls with mercury glass. In Easton's own Manhattan apartment, the mood is "very Regency . . . red-striped wallpaper, Directoire, that sort of thing."

Designing has been Easton's "sort of thing" since he roamed Marshall Field's antiques department in Chicago as a child visiting his grandparents. "I just fell in love," he says, simply. The degree he took some years later from Pratt was in architecture and design. Subsequently he went abroad to study European architecture in situ, then came back to New York to work with Edward Wormley, the legendary designer of interiors and furniture. Easton's final stop en route to establishing his own business was at Parish-Hadley Associates.

"I was searching for a way to incorporate my interest in interiors with my architectural design concerns," Easton says. Those concerns have grown increasingly classic, in accordance with the direction he sees the entire field taking in the future: "Design is becoming more dependent on classicism," he once told an interviewer. "Simpler, more subtle." □

The upholstered walls of the "Pavilion Room" are
hung with the client's collection of China trade paintings,
mostly from the eighteenth and nineteenth centuries.
In the foreground are a pair of French Empire chairs.

Opposite: Easton reordered the space in the dining room,
adding faux marble mouldings and pediments over
the doors to achieve a classical architectural
balance in the room.

Easton revived a favorite eighteenth-century design device: he added a false door to balance the architecture in the drawing room. Centered on a woven rug made after a French Empire design, the room features a set of four Louis XVI fauteuils and four eighteenth-century French ormolu wall sconces inset with Chinese porcelain plaques. The gilt mirror is George III.

"The past —
without duplicating the past"

EDWARD ZAJAC
RICHARD CALLAHAN

The mirrors they have designed over the years reflect the decorating philosophy of this fast-moving, fast-talking team.

Some, such as *La Pauline,* are named after people whose taste they admire, explains Edward Zajac. In this case it was the Baroness de Rothschild, née Pauline Potter, who inspired the three-part mirror that reappears several times in the designers' own East Village apartment-cum-studio. Another multifaceted mirror, with a name that translates roughly as *Snow Black and the Seven Dwarfs,* is typical of the sense of play that Zajac and Richard Callahan, his partner since 1964, bring to their history-rich decorative style.

Parsons-trained — they were classmates who toured the great houses of Europe with the school — they both apprenticed with classically oriented design firms before forming their own. Zajac spent nine years with the renowned Billy Baldwin; Callahan worked with Jansen, the French decorating firm.

Together they have evolved a look that, as Zajac expresses it, "acknowledges the past — without duplicating the past." He insists, "Not only do you need to know the past, you have to develop a sense of scale. . . . You have to know the work of Palladio in order to scale a lampshade properly." Many of their furnishings, in fact, are newly made, and though they may be designed with definite reference to historic sources, they are never copied, always original, and often amusing. A Chinese bed is a favorite document. Zajac and

Callahan have interpreted it for their own highly eclectic apartment, where it snuggles into a small sitting area under the carved eye of a Turkish bust atop a tall fluted column.

The same bed reappears in a client's dining room, piled with cushions and surrounded by six portraits of Indian rajahs, which the designers found on the Spanish Steps in Rome. In front of the sofa sits a gathering of red leather chairs, English Regency, dating from the 1840s. Across the room is a contemporary dining table set with dishes designed by Roy Lichtenstein. It is a merry mixture of moods, colors, and scale, drawn from many sources and orchestrated into surprising homogeneity by the designers' deft feeling for proportion.

"Proportion," observes Zajac, "is what separates the men from the boys. Lots of people have wonderful taste, but they can't pull off the scale."

In their practice, Callahan says, "we try to work like a painter would, moving things around, playing them against each other, arranging them like a still life. We've been called the 'more is more' decorators," he acknowledges with a smile.

"But we use what works," adds Zajac. "If Louis XIV had had it, he'd have used Formica and track lighting, too. You draw from the past, but you don't repeat it exactly. And that, I think, sums up our definition of Manhattan Style: it's high style, sophisticated and very American . . . not just another pretty room."

Stairs spiral up two more levels to the showroom, the designers' private quarters, and a vast outdoor garden overlooking the Hudson River. Inside, the stair landing is hung with art and brackets holding a classic bust and Chinese porcelains. The leaded-glass terrarium is Victorian.

The astonished-looking head is
Greek, from Turkey; it oversees a narrow
passage made bright with a mirror-studded
papier-mâché table designed by Zajac and
Callahan. Flanking it are a pair of nineteenth-
century gilt chairs from Russia.

Opposite: An amalgamation of mirrors makes
the most of the small sitting space that Zajac
and Callahan have carved out for themselves
in the converted West Village meat-packing
plant where they live and work. The gilt-
trimmed chairs, Chinese bed/sofa, and fabric
on the screens are all of their design.

A Louis XVI bed holds sway over the master bedroom, hung with embroidered lace and wrapped in plaid raw silk. English floral carpeting runs from wall to wall underneath.

Opposite: Reworking the architecture of a client's uptown apartment, Zajac and Callahan used French doors in place of windows to create the atmosphere of a villa, all airiness and serenity, based on bleached floors and set with surprises: a rock-crystal chimneypiece, Chinese garden stools, a Bristol mercury-glass chandelier. The nineteenth-century Chinese mother-of-pearl cabinet came from Rose Cumming.

The contemporary dining table is set with china designed by Roy Lichtenstein. The foyer beyond is deliberately evocative of Italy, say the decorators, who gave it a painted ceiling and a Venetian console table.

Opposite: In the dining/sitting room, contemporary track lighting spotlights the designers' signature sofa, inspired by a Chinese bed. Portraits of six Indian rajahs survey the eclectic scene, which includes English Regency chairs in red leather.

"A changing exhibition"

EDGAR MUNHALL

It was the gift of a lifetime, and it was to change home life dramatically for Edgar Munhall, Ph.D., curator of the Frick Collection, specialist in eighteenth-century French art, and, suddenly, owner of an extraordinary library supplementing his own collection of classics in French literature.

A friend bequeathed Munhall the contents of his library, some three thousand volumes in all. It was a staggering gift, all the more so because Munhall was living in a one-bedroom apartment with no intention of moving.

The solution: Munhall would sleep in the library, surrounded by shelves of books that now run from wall to wall and from floor to ceiling. Munhall has made the transformation from bedroom to *bibliothèque* work beautifully. Framed between wide mouldings and balanced by double sets of six-panel doors, the built-in shelves look indigenous to the room. The doors themselves are actually another splendid bit of legerdemain: one set is functional, leading to the next room, but the other merely backs a Parsons table on which Munhall displays photographs and *objets* in winter. In summer the table moves aside and the doors open to reveal a window.

Although the curator is a persistent collector — of art, faience, Renaissance medals, and, more recently, work by young photographers — losing four walls of display space to books posed no problem. He hangs relatively few artworks anyway, preferring to prop up current favorites on a narrow display shelf that runs at chair-rail height down one living-room wall. He is also likely to lean a framed piece in an odd corner or against

one wall of books in the bedroom–cum–reading room.

"I live with a changing exhibition of my own collection," Munhall explains. "When I keep them circulating this way, I see things afresh every time I bring them out." Which, he says, is apt to be whenever he "needs a visual jolt, about every six weeks or so."

Between viewings, the artworks are rotated back into Munhall's closet. There are several hundred pieces in all, ranging from contemporary photographs to works by Jean-Baptiste Greuze, the eighteenth-century French artist who has preoccupied much of Munhall's professional time since Yale — "I've spent most of my life writing a catalogue of his works," he says.

The rest of his time has been largely devoted to another extraordinary collection, the one amassed by Henry Clay Frick early in this century and housed in his Fifth Avenue mansion, now open as a museum. Climbing the splendid marble staircase every day, Munhall goes to work in what was once the Fricks' private family quarters, on the second floor of the mansion. His office, some forty by twenty-five feet of baronial splendor, was formerly Frick's own sitting room. Just outside is the long corridor with ceiling paintings by Alden Twachtman, executed at the direction of the decorator Elsie de Wolfe, whom Frick hired to furnish and decorate the family rooms.

His history-steeped, elegant surroundings are all in a day's work for Munhall: "My business hours are spent in such grandeur," he reflects, smiling, "it's nice to go home to my cozy little apartment." □

Against walls that Munhall describes as "Pompeiian red," a display shelf holds a changing exhibition of artworks and photographs, including a chalk drawing by Jean-Baptiste Greuze. The screen is nineteenth-century Chinese wallpaper; the rug, Indian.

Set off by a faux ostrich-skin screen, the marble dining table displays part of Munhall's collection of French and Italian faience, with pretend eggs, onions, salami, and olives mixed in with actual edibles. The engravings show two views of the arch of triumph erected to celebrate the arrival of Marie Antoinette in Versailles; the drawing is an illustration by Oudry for the *Fables* of La Fontaine.

Opposite: The ultimate room for reading in bed: Munhall's inherited library wraps around the bedroom walls. The double doors behind the table conceal a window.

"The collage of a lifetime"

TOM LACY

They have been together for some thirty years, Tom Lacy and his tiny Greenwich Village apartment. And at last, he says, he has given in to its nocturnal personality and learned how to decorate "in layers."

For the first decade he lived there, Lacy kept painting the apartment white. It was, he says now with a smile, "a desperate attempt to make it into a 'day' apartment." Besides, as a Parsons-trained graphic designer (his first career), he knew that wide expanses of white will push back walls and make spaces look larger. In theory.

In practice, it did not work. The tiny apartment is carved, in typical Greenwich Village fashion, out of the first floor of what was once a multiple-family dwelling. And Lacy is a relentless collector . . . of books, art, *objets,* and theater memorabilia, including costume designs and stage sets by such talents as Eugene Berman, Rex Whistler, and Leon Bakst, whose work for Diaghilev sparked the rage for the Oriental style early in this century.

"When the acquiring started, it was like opening the sluice gate," Lacy admits. "By now, this apartment has become the collage of my lifetime." The "collage" unfolds, layer upon layer, against a night-dark background. The walls are wrapped in black burlap; the ceiling and woodwork are painted rich black; dark glazed-chintz curtains occlude all the windows and are draped over the doorway between the two rooms.

"It always was a 'night' apartment, and I finally had to accept it," he says. He also realized that only an equally realistic approach would solve his acute shortage of space. So most of the walls are now given over to neatly ordered bookcases that run from floor to ceiling, pausing here and there to accommodate Lacy's desk or to frame one of the drawings done for him by Andy Warhol when they worked together in the advertising design department at Bonwit Teller.

Over the books hangs his collection of paintings and drawings — "This is the 'layered look' in decorating," he observes — but still the library functions: "I'm a Virgo, so my books are well organized, starting with fiction and running down through biography to sociology."

The books have stayed put even though Lacy's second career — in acting — has often taken him to the West Coast and sometimes kept him there for long periods. In addition to his Broadway and California stage work, he has done movie and television roles (including a nine-year stint as the jovial spokesman for Beefsteak Charlie's restaurant chain). He even bought a condo during one extended California stay, but this tiny, warm, dark "night" apartment has always meant *home* to him.

Lacy is, after all, a native of New York City, and as he puts it, "Home is where the books are." □

Over the desk is an original drawing for Andy Warhol's book *Wild Raspberries;* above it is a poster by Bérard. Down the right of the door frame, the illustrations are by Tchelitchew (*top*), Cecil Beaton, and Alexandre Benois; on the chair is a costume design by Eugene Berman for *Otello.*

Making the most of every precious inch in his small apartment, Tom Lacy has organized his library according to category and hung his paintings and drawings over the books in "layers."

Opposite: Lacy covered his walls in black burlap to create a background for his collection of set and costume designs. Above the mirror over the bed/sofa is a watercolor by Christian Bérard. A collection of Staffordshire dogs tops a Victorian table. The smaller table is a Saarinen design.

A window on Manhattan

GENE MOORE

Gene Moore doesn't have to tell you — with his mischievous grin — that he "does windows." The world has known that since 1955, when Moore became display director of Tiffany & Company and began creating designs in the five small windows that wrap around the corner of Fifth Avenue and Fifty-seventh Street.

More than four thousand inspired ideas later, those windows have become the most elegant "running street theater" in New York, and Gene Moore, long since named a vice president of the store, has been credited with elevating window dressing to new potency as both a retailing tool and an art form. Yet the wry septuagenarian emphasizes, "I haven't even gotten started!"

The inspiration that feeds the relentless demand for display ideas (Tiffany's windows are changed every two or three weeks) comes from "everywhere," Moore says. "It's all around you constantly, if you know how to see and not just look." Through Moore's magic, window-watchers have seen the mundane and the divine, often in amusing juxtaposition: diamonds and precious gems displayed against backgrounds of dirt, leaves, sand, pasta, empty thread spools, and ice cream cones. Visual puns and gentle satire are Moore's signatures. Once, during a water shortage in New York, Moore filled a tiny fountain with gin ("The whole first floor of the store smelled like a martini for two weeks," he remembers, chuckling with delight).

Tiffany gives Moore carte blanche for his windows: the idea comes first and selling the merchandise second. But his displays attract buyers as well as admirers. Moore loves that. If something in the window is sold, "it might ruin the display," he says, "but then we are not here for the sake of art."

Artists are another matter. Moore has commissioned work from some eight hundred over the years, including Robert Rauschenberg, Jasper Johns, and Andy Warhol. Moore himself is no slouch in the fine arts, either. A native of Birmingham, Alabama, who studied at the Chicago Academy of Fine Arts, he arrived in New York intent on painting. A succession of unlikely jobs came first, however: delivery boy for a religious publishing house, busboy in a cafeteria, waiter on a cruise ship to South America. His first work in display was at I. Miller; Bergdorf Goodman was next, then Bonwit Teller, and then Tiffany. Between windows he has designed costumes and sets for the Paul Taylor Dance Company, for Sir John Gielgud in London, and for several off-Broadway productions in New York. "In the theater, you get to work *large*," says the designer.

Moore has also designed the Christmas trees at the landmark Seagram Building, turning the fountain areas into an evergreen forest covered with tiny white lights and launching a seasonal trend in the process. He once decorated Mount Vernon for a party given by President and Mrs. Kennedy and more recently created his own circus for Tiffany, with three rings' worth of silver and enamel animals and performers just inches high.

In Moore's own apartment, near the United Nations building, his talent as a sculptor is writ large in tiny table vignettes that feature other animals he has designed: zebras made of white gold touched with diamonds, eighteen-karat-gold deer, tigers with emerald eyes. Sculpture and paintings by other artists occupy any wall space not given over to the twenty-eight-foot-long bookshelves Moore had built ("I couldn't live without my books!" he exclaims).

Warm, witty, and rich in visual serendipities, the apartment is an extension of its owner's definition of Manhattan Style: "Do anything you want. Be original. In other cities, people tend to copy. Not here. In New York, people want to be different."   □

No surprise for a master of display, Moore's entry hall features a wall-sized "vignette": a horn table and mirror are displayed against the wallpaper forest.

Opposite: The greatest little show on earth plays the dinner-party circuit in Moore's apartment. He created the silver and enamel circus figures for Tiffany & Company. The dishes and glasses, also from Tiffany, were designed by Van Day Truex when he was design director for the store.

Art Deco revisited

KARL SPRINGER

For many years the designer Karl Springer carried a torch for Art Deco, rejoicing in its classic simplicity of line and its fabulously rich, often exotic finishes long after fashion had moved on. Today he could be called the bearer of the flame for thirties design, now that it has come full circle back into vogue.

Certainly Springer's interpretations are high on the list for other designers seeking Art Deco elegance for their clients. Furnishings with a design heritage traceable to Emile-Jacques Ruhlmann and light fixtures inspired by Perzel cast a decidedly thirties glow over the offerings in the showrooms of Karl Springer, Limited, worldwide. Art Deco touches also pervade the antiqued copper-leafed rooms in Springer's own apartment, some forty stories above the East Side skyline. But equally evident are myriad other influences from many eras and many places: Africa, the Orient, the Bauhaus period in his native Germany, and, also from France of the 1930s, the spare, elegant, enduring classics of Jean-Michel Frank.

Springer came to New York from Berlin in 1957, a young man with a great appetite for old-world craftsmanship. He applied it first to the art of bookbinding, apprenticing himself to learn leather-working techniques. Quickly, however, he began developing his own methods for covering other kinds of objects in fine leathers and skins. Then several watershed developments sent him on his way to the international acclaim he enjoys today: Bergdorf-Goodman bought his work and introduced it to an influential clientele; the renowned Billy Baldwin asked him to re-create a parchment table that had been originally designed in the 1920s by Jean-Michel Frank; the Duchess of Windsor became an admirer, collecting the small, leather-covered telephone tables by Springer that moved about on casters.

A rich interplay of textures: a natural narwhal tusk and a sculpture, *Sun*, by the Munich artist Burkhard Backe. The Springer-designed sofa has palisander arms and is covered in a fabric derivative of the Bauhaus. The table is a nineteenth-century African tribal stool topped with glass.

As he says now with a laugh, "With that blessing from the Duchess, I could have gone on making those little phone tables forever." They are still a popular item in the Springer line, but as the jovial, urbane designer has said, "You need a challenge in life."

His challenge has been to revive — and carry forward — the ancient technique of veneering, using such rich woods as palisander and bird's-eye maple (which lines his entire bedroom closet) and a menagerie of leathers: lizard, alligator, even frog, and goatskin so highly lacquered that it emulates marble. Springer's team of artisans — sought out from around the world and under constant supervision by Karl and his brother Joachim — also works in granite and glass, fossilized coral, wrapping paper, stainless steel, and shagreen, real sharkskin.

His own preoccupation ("You could say 'obsession'!" he exclaims) with finishes is manifested in Springer's apartment from the doorway on. Once done all in sleek gray, the walls and ceilings have now been reclad in copper leaf — an idea he brought home, he says, after visiting a temple in Kyoto. In a dramatic refiguring of the space leading up to the spectacular view from the sitting-dining room, Springer has made the entry dark and tunnel-like, with mysteriously curving walls and lighting that is theatrical but subdued. Often it emanates from an unexpected source: from the illuminated base under an immense sixteenth-century Italian safe studded with wrought iron; from a curve of light edging the Lucite bedhead; from the reflective copper ceiling over the dining table.

That table, veneered in palisander (as is the Springer-designed sofa), is what he calls his "tribute to Ruhlmann." Similarly, the wall sconces in the living room are Springer's interpretations of two originals he owns by Perzel, who worked in the thirties and forties.

"I may be inspired by other designers, but the interpretations are strictly my own," Springer says. So is the choice of finishing materials, as well as the lifelong commitment to meticulous craftsmanship and detailing that, as he observes, "you could contemplate for hours."

Springer has achieved his ideal on a large scale in his skyscraping apartment. The overall glow of the copper leafing makes it seem "like being inside a little jewel box. When I had it all in gray, all sleek, it was cold and dark, always eight o'clock at night," he says. "Now the mood changes constantly. I love that." □

Opposite: An eighteenth-century Japanese screen bought in Kyoto covers one wall in the dining area. The copper ceiling reflects the table Springer designed as a "tribute to Ruhlmann"; the chairs are Chinese, circa seventeenth century.

Right: Against the allover glow from the copper-leafed ceiling and walls are drawings by José Maria Sert, cartoons for the murals he was to paint in 1937 for the main entrance of Rockefeller Plaza. Springer had the ebony desk made for himself after an Art Deco original in glass.

Living the "golden section"

ANDRÉ EMMERICH

Because art is essential to the life of noted gallery owner André Emmerich, so is a small can of spackle.

His collection at home is constantly on the move — "Rearranging art gives it a freshness," he maintains — and he keeps the spackle, as well as a tiny can of dead-white paint, always at hand to touch up the walls.

"One of the best things to do with an art collection is to move it around," observes the tall, Dutch-born Emmerich. A third-generation art dealer, he has, through his namesake gallery, handled many of the emerging new American and European talents of the past three decades. Over the years, the gallery has been among the most important sources for New York designers, who follow Elsie de Wolfe's lead in mixing contemporary art with venerable antiques. Where she hung Léger and Picasso — shocking and new in her era — today's designers might juxtapose an eighteenth-century French commode and, say, a David Hockney or a Helen Frankenthaler painting.

Emmerich goes home to both in his Upper East Side apartment. Frankenthaler's *Oceanus* hangs over the sofa; a David Hockney occupies the wall-to-wall niche in the dining area, where a Roman torso of Venus is silhouetted against a view of Central Park, spread out far below. Opposite Venus is an Attic amphora from the sixth century B.C. All through the apartment, contemporary sculpture by some of André Emmerich's personal favorites — among them Anthony Caro and Beverly Pepper — coexists peaceably with *objets* from another genre that fascinates him, pre-Columbian art.

Emmerich wrote the book on the latter, quite literally. An accomplished journalist before he succumbed to an overriding interest in art, he has published two books and continues to write a number of scholarly articles on pre-Columbian art.

Also an authority on contemporary art, Emmerich says that his own collection is drawn from two constantly changing sources: "Some are masterpieces, things I simply didn't want to lose"; other pieces in his collection are either gifts or have sentimental value. Whatever the source, the apartment has taken on the calm of an art gallery. The furnishings are understated, the colors subdued. Displayed against walls of "photographer's white," the art is the raison d'être.

The business of art itself has grown dramatically during the decades he has been observing it firsthand, says Emmerich. "In 1954 [the year he opened his gallery], the art scene was a very small world. The number of people in it was small . . . certainly, the numbers for which art sold were much smaller. Today, both have become enormous."

But even "enormous" figures cannot always buy good taste, Emmerich knows. Take the matter of small occasional tables. He could find neither a cocktail table nor bedside tables to please his practiced eye, so he simply sat down and designed his own, applying that classical equation which governs proportions, known as the "golden section." Rendered in rosewood and glass, versions of the cocktail table now reside in Emmerich's Fifty-seventh Street gallery as well. They are handsome testimony to his definition of taste: "You can be born with an eye for art, just as one is born with an ear for music. But to truly develop an eye is like the building of character . . . it takes time and practice." □

Emmerich framed David Hockney's *Midnight Pool* as a triptych to fit in the niche over a marble dining table. It is surrounded by four of six Italian Directoire chairs. On her pedestal *(left)*, the torso of Venus is Roman, dating from the first or second century B.C.

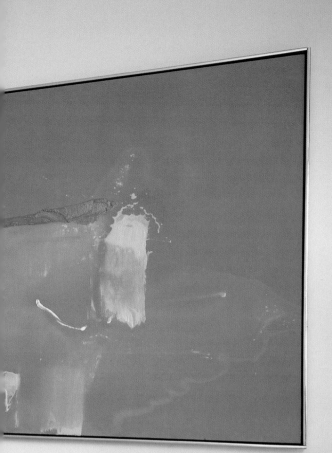

The collector's personal collection: artworks in Emmerich's study/dressing room include a watercolor by Sheila Girling, on the radiator in front of a Helen Frankenthaler, and a sixteenth-century majolica plate over a painting by Larry Poons (*at lower right*). A late-eighteenth-century Italian tub chair is drawn up to an early-nineteenth-century Austrian Biedermeier desk; the chair at right is English, circa 1790.

Opposite: On the cocktail table, which André Emmerich designed himself, is *Silver Piece 21*, by Anthony Caro. *Oceanus*, painted by Helen Frankenthaler in 1981, covers the wall behind the sofa. To its left is Kenneth Noland's *Coal*.

The calm of no color

JAMES E. GOSLEE III

A celebrated party stylist whose colorful fantasies last one spectacular night only, Jim Goslee delights in coming home to his fourth-floor walk-up in Greenwich Village and to the perennial white at the top of the stairs.

Goslee will smile and tell you that he gives parties for a living. His definition falls short. What Goslee does for the well-known and the well-to-do across the country is to create party atmospheres that are, in his words, "larger than life, designed to light up all the senses and last just one night."

The designer, who pursued architecture and graphic design at Pratt after studying photography and painting at Parsons, has been called a "floral architect" by the *New York Times*. You will not find that on his business card, however, even though he did own a Manhattan flower shop at one time and relandscaped the White House Rose Garden for President Ford. Now he works in many other media as well, from computer-controlled lighting to scented oils for burning when he sets out to create a total "atmosphere" for, say, New York's Museum of Natural History (where he used lights and real sand to conjure up an undersea mood beneath the belly of the museum's famed blue whale).

His ephemeral, often flamboyant "atmospheres" have made Goslee sought-after by party planners on both coasts: cross-continent flights, his luggage filled with fresh flowers and personal props, are all in a day's work. But for its creator the party ends when the first guests arrive,

"which is usually just as I light the last candle after working through the previous night and day to get ready," he says.

Home, he is quick to add, has become a welcome refuge from a professional life lived with stopwatch in hand, surrounded by high-energy color and pure fantasy. "I need to come home to quiet, to comfort and my personal things," the southern-born Goslee confirms. His Village studio, now partially partitioned to create a sliver of a separate bedroom, is a study in black and white — "my colors," he says. White walls run up to the black-framed skylight and down to a black carpet under a black-and-white cowhide. The sailcloth covers on the deep, many-cushioned sofa and the director's chairs are white; so are the few cabinets and most of the accessories. Even the artworks — all by friends, including Richard Giglio — are predominantly in black and white.

Still, there is no lack of colorful touches, such as Goslee's collection of palm trees, both miniature, in metal, and growing live ("I have a thing about palms — they're a fantasy, an Orientalist, Eastern thing," he explains). And there is more than a hint of whimsy in the stackable/restackable table made of textured butcher blocks, and in the fancifully turned and painted Victorian table that he brought home from a flea market.

"The talent is to be able to mix the ordinary and the extraordinary, Azuma with Woolworth's with great things," Goslee observes. "People who have their own great sense of style also have the courage to mix." □

A rearrangeable arrangement: stackable butcher blocks hold the designer's highly personal collection of shapes — "I love triangles and palm trees," he says. The sculpture head once belonged to the English designer David Hicks.

The bed runs wall-to-wall in the tiny sleeping area
that Goslee created by adding a partial wall (*at left*). It
stops short of the clerestory, leaving the entire apartment
open to the New York sky.

Opposite: A study in black and white, Jim Goslee's fourth-
floor studio is wide open to the view of Greenwich Village
treetops. Even the artwork carries forth the
non-color scheme.

Space...in eight shades of white

JACK CEGLIC
FOR
JOEL DEAN

Jack Ceglic still shakes his head in wonder at the furor he caused back in 1969, when he created what turned out to be *the* prototype inner-city loft apartment. The four-thousand-square-foot, one-room loft in a turn-of-the-century toy factory presented brave new life-style possibilities, especially for New Yorkers caught in their eternal quest for living space.

Behind the bleak facades of warehouses looming over narrow cobblestone streets in SoHo — the area south of Houston Street — there was, as Tom Wolfe might put it, SPACE, almighty, AF-FORDABLE S-P-A-C-E so big it almost offered vanishing-point perspective!

And the artist Jack Ceglic showed how to make it sleek, elegant, open, an interior landscape so roomy that the grand piano seemed a mere accessory. Photographs of the loft popped up in publications all over the United States, in Europe, and even in Japan.

"It never occurred to me that I would be inventing a prototype," recalls Ceglic now, smiling. At the time, he says, he was really just looking "for a place to live and work" as a Parsons-trained fashion illustrator–turned–painter. Ceglic's talents spread to store design when Joel Dean and Giorgio DeLuca started their first, small Dean & DeLuca specialty foods store up the street from his loft. Legendary even in a city where food is the object of fanaticism and gourmet shops appear on every other corner, the store itself has also become a prototype, its loftlike openness and merchandise "vignettes" copied all over the country.

"We 'merchandise' the store," Ceglic says. "It's the same principles you apply to making an effective poster: you have to edit with your eyes so things read very fast."

Mastering the principle took the native New Yorker from Parsons to such high-fashion stores as Bonwit Teller and the now defunct B. Altman and Arnold Constable. Then the other fine arts took over: painting, interior design, and even landscaping.

"Landscaping is like doing a large loft. You have sightlines, perspectives, and vanishing points outside, and inside [too] when the space is this big," he explains, squinting across the gleaming white-painted floors to the sixty-foot-long bookshelves that line one wall. Two others are given over to the large windows — seventeen in all — that once shed light on the toy-makers' efforts and now flood the room with sunshine. The miniblinds are seldom lowered; by a happy coincidence, the windows opposite both sleeping areas and the walk-through bath were already glazed with opaque glass.

There are no inner walls, unless you count the ten-foot-plus closets that define the bath, and the curved partition that arches around the shower. Both are backed with large paintings by Ceglic, but neither inhibits the on-flow of space, all of it in white — there are seven or eight different shades of white in the loft, Ceglic points out, ranging from cool to warm, from matte to gloss. Against the subtle monochrome, every object in the loft takes on shibui-like importance.

"That's why I like to buy for other people," the artist confides. "At home, even with all this space, I have to restrain myself." □

Meals on wheels: the kitchen work counter is on rollers so it can float up to serve the dining table that came with the loft. Once a work table in the former toy factory, it is covered with ordinary floorboards and surrounded by leather Mexican café chairs.

A sixty-foot library of art books and records backs another sleeping area. Behind the column, vent pipes become a decorative element in the walk-through bath. The ratchet sofa, like all the upholstered furniture in the loft, is covered in a raincoat material that Ceglic bought for a dime a yard on Delancey Street. The paintings are both by him.

Opposite: Some eight different shades of white lend subtle definition to the four-thousand-square-foot SoHo loft. One "open-air" seating area is demarcated by the brown leather Stickley daybed, marked and dated 1904. The white sofa, a bed by night, floor-sits behind a table that Ceglic found on the curb. The worm-eaten turned stool dates from the Tudor period; the Westport garden chair in the far distance was made in 1905.

RENNY REYNOLDS

Downstairs, on the street level of the four-story town house, the air is always fragrant with blossoms — and slightly super-charged. Someone somewhere in New York is having a party, and everyone at Renny the Florist is working against a perennial deadline, fashion-ing elegant floral displays and organizing room "transformations" for clients as diverse as the Metropolitan Museum of Art and, in the old days, Studio 54.

Upstairs, however, quiet prevails. Far removed from the social whirl that he helps to set in mo-tion, Renny Reynolds lives above the store, in an apartment centered around a glassed-over open courtyard. From the courtyard rises the constant music of a running fountain and the fresh breath of green, growing things. The apartment comes close to having one foot in the country, an emo-tional prerequisite for the St. Louis–born Reyn-olds, who studied landscape architecture and urban and regional planning at the University of Wisconsin.

For the past twenty years, much of his land-scaping has been done indoors, usually on table-tops. Design for Entertaining, Reynolds's party-design company, is celebrated for creating "room transformations" that are dramatic yet refined. Most of these are large-scale productions, and not all unfold in New York. The company performs its party magic across the country, relying on leger-demain with color and lighting, as well as with flowers, to perfect the illusion.

Reynolds sees these creations as being of a piece with designing a room: "Everything — background, tablecloths, napkins and how they're folded — must add up to the illusion you're after." □

Right: Reynolds had a window made for an upstairs hall by combining glass taken from windows in a Connecticut school. The terra-cotta urns are from the nineteenth century; the Chinese dragon table is bronze and iron.

Opposite: Dining alfresco indoors: the table setting is readily at hand for a dinner party. A painted garden settee pulls up to a stone table on the first floor of the East Side town house, which Reynolds has renovated into an indoor garden, complete with a running fountain in the skylit atrium.

Stepping *in* to an English garden: customers and visitors at Renny Reynolds's town house find the first floor as fresh as all outdoors. Reynolds created faux stone walls inset with architectural arches and a floor of old brick interspersed with glass blocks. Both the pedestal urns and the wire garden chairs are English.

With one foot in an ancient world

JOHN SALADINO

The artist, architect, and designer John Saladino may believe, as he quotes, that "God is in the details." But don't look for perfection in a Saladino-designed room. The altar at which he pays homage will be deliberately imperfect, time-worn and crumbling, perhaps covered with lichen, a relic from some ancient civilization, unnameable because it exists only in his mind's eye.

"Perfection is too slick," Saladino declares. Nonetheless, he can be a perfectionist about the historical illusions in his work, once going so far as to tint his trademark scratch-coat plaster walls with instant coffee to make them appear lichen-covered and ancient. Interiors that look naturally weathered are "more suggestive, more evocative," he maintains. That also explains his penchant for furniture with faded, worn painted finishes, and for luminous, illusive colors.

The artist in Saladino delights in the iridescent palette that has become another signature. His colors, he says, are "more cerebral than sensual." Now violet, now amethyst, now celadon, they meld and change with the light and angle.

The architect in Saladino (he holds a degree from the Yale School of Art and Architecture and launched his career in Rome) inspires constant reference to the classical past he knows so well. Those allusions, however, are always implicit, never explicit: a hint of Herculaneum here, an echo of Pompeii there, overtones of Renaissance Venice or the Temple at Karnak. Even his business card uses a typeface adopted from the Column of Trajan, he confides with a smile.

The designer in Saladino strives to evoke drama even as he endorses human scale and comfort. He likes to use opposites to "create sensuality: old with new, soft with hard, corroded with shiny. Dyna-metrically opposed, they infuse one another with new life. . . . Good design has to do with exaggerating the juxtaposition of things. An Adam sideboard against a concrete wall is a new experience. I consider myself an editor, sifting through a plethora of visual experiences. A room is never completed, or final, merely a fragment in a time continuum."

Saladino also likes to work in deliberate — sometimes dizzying — overscale to "alter the perception of scale [and] blur the boundaries between interior and exterior spaces. . . . I'm interested in illusion. That is what interior design is anyway," he has said.

The emotional impact of Saladino's rooms is very real, however, and it is one reason his work appeals both to modern tastes and to traditionalists. "I like to think of interior design as a fine art . . . something that goes beyond shelter and comfort," he once stressed in an interview. "I am not interested in living in a machine. I feel a dwelling should provoke an emotional response. There should be a sense of theater — a little pageantry."

He finds both in the classical themes he employs. "Consider an Italian carved wooden door, for example," Saladino explains. "It pays homage to the human being.

"Then think about a late twentieth-century door: it will be made of metal. And there will be a panic bar."

He continues musing: "Other generations understood the ceremony of living. In fact, there was so much taste right up to the First World War. That cracked the hulk. The Second World War sank it.

"And of all the things that once fed our hunger for ritual in life," he concludes quietly, "only the dining room is left to us."   □

Evoking the calm of the past in a client's entryway, John Saladino covered the walls in scratch-coat plaster and laid floors of silver travertine marble, installed on the diagonal. The console is also of Italian marble and dates from the late eighteenth century. Providing contrast and shine are glazed ceilings and a "Ya Ya Ho" halogen light.

Playing with scale on a grand scale, Saladino superimposes a nine-foot-tall column over an elevator shaft. It creates a startling vista from the dining room, which is done in tender greens and pinks, with Venetian overtones.

Opposite: In the drawing room, classic mouldings frame walls so pale they tend to change color with the light — a favorite bit of Saladino legerdemain. He designed the mirrored vitrine; the early-nineteenth-century screen unfolds for eighteen feet down one wall. It is French, covered in wallpaper that depicts a Chinese landscape. The painted chairs are Italian, from the eighteenth century.

In Saladino's own bed-sitting room, he covered the walls in paneling with a lacquer finish and added eighteenth-century Italian rock-crystal sconces. The chaises are European, also from the eighteenth century.

Opposite: In the soaring space of his drawing room — once Jay Gould's ballroom — the designer evokes an ambience of agreeable decay, reminiscent of an Italian villa. The walls are scratch-coat plaster; the leather chairs are from the seventeenth century. Power Boothe made the large painting on the far wall; Saladino himself, the painting at right.

Above: For a penthouse with a spectacular outlook on Central Park, Saladino opened up a bedroom with double-pane glass and heated the tile floors. (The bath, also under glass, is adjacent to the bedroom, with the tub elevated to take advantage of the view.) The pedestal table is Biedermeier.

Opposite: Downstairs in the duplex penthouse, space flows serenely between rooms in which Saladino's palette has been designed to "metamorphose" with the changing light. His signature chairs are juxtaposed with a mixture of antiques, including the eighteenth-century French bench in the living room, and contemporary art.

A doorway to the classical past: in his own apartment, John Saladino frames a view of the bed-sitting room with walls covered with scratch-coat plaster and hung with a quilt edged in leather piping. The "Tube Lamp" on the table is of his design; the chairs are English Hepplewhite, from the eighteenth century.

NOTES

1. Stephen Jones, "Understated Style," *Country Life,* June 8, 1989, 292.
2. Barbara Weinberg, Ph.D., "The Gilded Age: New York Places and Patrons," lecture at the National Academy of Design, New York City, January 6, 1989.
3. William A. Coles, "The Genesis of a Classic," introduction to Edith Wharton and Ogden Codman, Jr., *The Decoration of Houses* (reprint, New York: Classical America Series in Art and Architecture, W. W. Norton, 1978), xxxi.
4. Ibid., xxvii.
5. Diana Vreeland, preface to Jane S. Smith, *Elsie de Wolfe, A Life in the High Style* (New York: Atheneum, 1982), xi.
6. Billy Baldwin, "The Importance of Rooms People Live In," *House & Garden,* October 1970, 8.
7. Jane S. Smith, *Elsie de Wolfe,* 135.
8. Richard Guy Wilson, "Edith and Ogden: Writing, Decorating, and Architecture," in *Ogden Codman and the Decoration of Houses* (Boston: Boston Athenaeum/David R. Godine, 1989), 155–156.
9. Van Day Truex, "Jean-Michel Frank Remembered," *Architectural Digest,* September/October 1976, 71.
10. Jean Cocteau, quoted in C. Ray Smith, *Interior Design in Twentieth-Century America: A History* (New York: Harper & Row, 1987), 138.
11. Truex, "Jean-Michel Frank Remembered," 75.
12. C. Ray Smith, *Interior Design,* 190.
13. Billy Baldwin, quoted in Christopher Hemphill, "Tastemakers: Van Day Truex," *House & Garden,* March 1984, 51–52.
14. C. Ray Smith, *Interior Design,* 99.
15. Cecil Beaton, *The Glass of Fashion* (Garden City, N.Y.: Doubleday, 1954), 247.
16. Billy Baldwin with Michael Gardine, *Billy Baldwin: An Autobiography* (Boston: Little, Brown, 1985), 129.
17. Eleanor McMillen, quoted in C. Ray Smith, *Interior Design,* 100.
18. Billy Baldwin, quoted in *Women's Wear Daily,* May 25, 1964, 4.

BIBLIOGRAPHY

Baldwin, Billy. *Billy Baldwin Decorates.* New York: Holt, Rinehart, and Winston, 1972.

———. *Billy Baldwin Remembers.* New York: Harcourt Brace Jovanovich, 1974.

———. "Decorating in This Century." *House & Garden Decorating Guide,* Spring 1981.

———. "The Importance of Rooms People Live In." *House & Garden,* October 1970.

Baldwin, Billy, with Michael Gardine. *Billy Baldwin: An Autobiography.* Boston: Little, Brown, 1985.

Barrows, Stanley. "Stanley Barrows on Disciplined Design." *Architectural Digest,* October 1981.

———. "Stanley Barrows on Memorable Design." *Architectural Digest,* September 1981.

Beaton, Cecil. *The Glass of Fashion.* Garden City, N.Y.: Doubleday, 1954.

Behrman, S. N. *Duveen.* New York: Random House, 1952.

Brown, Erica. *Sixty Years of Interior Design: The World of McMillen.* New York: Viking, 1982.

Canatsey, Christopher, and Susan Watters. "David Easton's Design for Living." *W,* April 3, 1989.

Chanaux, Adolphe. *Jean-Michel Frank.* Paris: Editors du Regard, 1980.

"The Decorating Art of Lady Mendl." *House & Garden,* May 1941.

de Wolfe, Elsie. *After All.* New York: Harper & Brothers, 1935.

———. *The House in Good Taste.* New York: Century, 1920.

Duka, John. "Behind Angelo Donghia's Gray-Flannel Success." *New York Times,* January 20, 1983.

Fisher, Richard B. *Syrie Maugham.* London: Gerald Duckworth & Co., 1978.

Fowler, John, and John Cornforth. *English Decoration in the Eighteenth Century.* London: Barrie & Jenkins, 1983.

Geniesse, Jane. "Van Truex: Designer and Catalyst." *New York Times,* November 16, 1978.

Green, Robert L. "The Legendary Ruby Ross Wood." *Architectural Digest,* October 1979.

Hemphill, Christopher. "Van Day Truex." *House & Garden,* March 1984.

"The Influence of William Odom on American Taste." *House & Garden,* July 1946.

Jones, Stephen. "Understated Style." *Country Life,* June 8, 1989.

Kornbluth, Jesse. "Angelo Donghia: Interior Designer As Superstar." *Metropolitan Home,* April 1981.

Lawford, Valentine. "An Interview with Billy Baldwin." *Architectural Digest,* September 1977.

———. "Le Style Pauline." *Vogue,* October 1966.

Metcalf, Pauline C., ed. *Ogden Codman and the Decoration of Houses.* Boston: Boston Athenaeum/David R. Godine, 1989.

Parsons, Frank Alvah. *Interior Decoration, Its Principles and Practice.* New York: Doubleday, Page & Co., 1916.

Pool, Mary Jane, ed. *Twentieth-Century Decorating, Architecture & Gardens: Eighty Years of Ideas and Pleasure from House & Garden.* New York: Holt, Rinehart, and Winston, 1980.

Richardson, John. "The Life and Times of 'Mr. Taste.'" *House & Garden,* April 1976.

Richardson, Nancy. "Elsie de Wolfe." *House & Garden,* April 1982.

Smith, C. Ray. *Interior Design in Twentieth-Century America: A History.* New York: Harper & Row, 1987.

Smith, Jane S. *Elsie de Wolfe: A Life in the High Style.* New York: Atheneum, 1982.

Truex, Van Day. "Jean-Michel Frank Remembered." *Architectural Digest,* September/October 1976.

———. "Responsibility in Design." *Architectural Digest,* September 1977.

Tweed, Katherine, ed. *The Finest Rooms by America's Great Decorators.* New York: Bramhall House, 1964.

Varney, Carleton. *The Draper Touch.* New York: Prentice Hall, 1988.

Wharton, Edith. *A Backward Glance.* New York: Scribner's, 1933.

Wharton, Edith, and Ogden Codman, Jr. *The Decoration of Houses.* 1897. Reprint. New York: Norton, 1978.

Wright, Richardson. *House & Garden's Book of Interiors.* New York: Conde Nast, 1920.

INDEX